Tarun Gupta

The Man Who Taught Marketing to the Indian Pharmaceutical Industry

Tarun Gupta (1939—2017)

Tarun Gupta

The Man Who Taught Marketing to the Indian Pharmaceutical Industry

Subba Rao Chaganti

PharmaMed Press™

An imprint of BSP Books Pvt. Ltd.
4-4-309/316, Giriraj Lane,
Sultan Bazar, Hyderabad - 500 001,
Telangana, India.

Tarun Gupta: The Man who taught Marketing to the Indian Pharmaceutical Industry
by Subba Rao Chaganti

Published by

PharmaMed Press™

An imprint of BSP Books Pvt. Ltd.
4-4-309/316, Giriraj Lane, Sultan Bazar,
Hyderabad - 500 001, Telangana, India.
Phone: 040-23445688
E-mail: info@pharmamedpress.net
www.bspbooks.net/www.pharmamedpress.net

ISBN: 978-93-47311-76-5 (Paperback)

Disclaimer

This book is an interpretive, narrative account of the life, work, and influence of Dr. Tarun Gupta, as well as the evolution of pharmaceutical marketing in India over several decades. It has been written with the objective of documenting ideas, systems, leadership practices, and professional standards that shaped an industry, rather than providing an exhaustive or definitive historical record.

The material presented in this book is derived from a combination of publicly available sources, industry publications, archival material, obituaries and public tributes, and professional recollection, including the author's own experience of working and learning under Dr. Tarun Gupta's tutelage during the formative period of his career. While every reasonable effort has been made to ensure accuracy, balance, and fairness, it is acknowledged that not all facts, events, or perspectives may be fully represented, and that some important details or viewpoints may be absent or underemphasized.

Certain incidents, decisions, timelines, and anecdotes described in this book rely on memory and shared professional narratives that have evolved over time. As such, they may be subject to limitations of recall, interpretation, or availability of documentation. The author does not claim absolute completeness or infallibility, nor does this work purport to represent the official position, views, or records of any organization, institution, or individual referenced.

This book is not an authorized biography. References to companies, brands, institutions, products, or individuals are made strictly for educational, historical, and illustrative purposes. No endorsement, affiliation, or sponsorship is implied.

The intent of this work is constructive documentation, not final adjudication of history. Readers who believe that important factual corrections, clarifications, or additional perspectives should be considered are encouraged to share such information with the author. Where appropriate and verifiable, such inputs may be reviewed and considered for inclusion in future editions.

Any errors of fact, omission, or interpretation remain the responsibility of the author alone.

This book is intended for general informational and educational purposes only and should not be construed as professional, legal, or commercial advice.

Author's Note

This book grew out of proximity as much as observation.

In the formative years of my career, I had the privilege of working and learning under Tarun Gupta's tutelage. I grew, not because I was encouraged, but because I was held to standards. Thinking had to be clear. Execution had to be disciplined. Explanations had to withstand scrutiny. Over time, those expectations shaped how I understood marketing, leadership, and responsibility.

Years later, as I engaged with professionals across the Indian pharmaceutical industry—as a teacher, writer, and observer—I noticed something striking. Individuals who had never worked together often shared the same grammar of thinking. When traced back, that grammar almost always led to one source: TG.

This book is an attempt to understand how that influence took shape.

It is not an authorized biography, nor is it intended as a definitive history. It is an interpretive account of how ideas, systems, and standards were introduced, taught, and carried forward—often without formal ownership. My interest lies less in chronology than in method: how experience was translated into structure, and structure into habit.

In writing this book, I have drawn on publicly available sources, industry publications, archival material, and professional memory—my own and that of others who worked with or learned from TG. Many episodes described here have existed for decades as shared professional narratives. Where facts could be verified, they have been. Where memory fills gaps, it is presented with restraint and transparency.

This book is written with respect, but not reverence. TG himself resisted elevation and distrusted certainty. He valued questioning over agreement, judgment over doctrine, and practice over proclamation. I have tried to honor that spirit by focusing on the systems he built, the standards he enforced, and the thinking he insisted upon—rather than on personal acclaim.

Attention is also paid to restraint. Decisions not taken, opportunities declined, and limits imposed are treated here as expressions of leadership, not omissions. In my experience, these moments reveal character more clearly than success alone.

Any errors of fact or interpretation remain my responsibility. This work is offered in the spirit of documentation, not finality, and remains open to correction and refinement.

If this book succeeds, it will not be because it captures a life in full, but because it preserves a way of thinking—one that treated marketing as a discipline, leadership as responsibility, and learning as unfinished work.

Subba Rao Chaganti

Acknowledgements

This book could not have been written without the generosity of memory, reflection, and example offered—directly and indirectly—by many individuals who shaped, witnessed, and carried forward Tarun Gupta's influence.

First and foremost, this work is a tribute to Dr. Tarun Gupta himself. While he may never have set out to create a legacy, he lived in a way that made one inevitable. His insistence on clarity over comfort, discipline over display, and practice over proclamation continues to shape how pharmaceutical marketing is understood and practiced in India. This book attempts to honor not just what he did, but how he thought.

I am deeply indebted to the many former colleagues, students, and protégés of TG — often referred to, with quiet affection, as the TG Tribe. Through conversations, recollections, shared anecdotes, and lived examples, they helped surface patterns that no archive could capture. Their careers stand as living footnotes to the narrative presented here.

My sincere thanks to Anil Shah, the publisher, for believing in the importance of documenting this story and for supporting its journey from concept to completion. I am equally grateful to Nikunjesh Shah, whose commitment ensured that the digital editions of this book would be accessible to a wider audience, extending its reach beyond print and geography.

I would like to acknowledge Naresh Davergave and his dedicated team at PharmaMed Press, whose design sensibility, editorial care, and production rigor gave this book its final form. Their work reflects the same discipline and respect for craft that Tarun Gupta himself championed.

I also acknowledge with respect the institutions that provided the arenas in which TG's ideas took root and spread—Boots, Glaxo, Burroughs Wellcome, and later JBIMS and NMIMS. These organizations were more than employers or classrooms; they were laboratories in which systems were tested, refined, and taught forward.

This book also draws strength from the broader Indian pharmaceutical industry, which absorbed, adapted, and evolved TG's ideas over decades. That an entire industry could be shaped by systems rather than slogans is a testament to its openness to learning and professionalism.

On a deeply personal note, I am grateful to my family, whose presence makes sustained intellectual work possible. To my spouse, Mahalakshmi, for her patience and quiet encouragement; to my children and their spouses — Srinivasa Phanindra, Geetha, Lavanya, Satya Sankara Aditya, Sowmya, and Chaitanya — for their constant support and belief; and to my grandchildren — Aditi, Eesha, Surya, and Shriya — who remind me, in the most human way, why ideas, values, and examples must be carried forward across generations.

I also acknowledge the readers — students, practitioners, leaders, and educators — who continue to seek depth in a field often reduced to tactics. This book exists because there is a community that believes marketing, when practiced responsibly, can elevate both business and society.

Finally, a note on intent. This is not an official history, nor an authorized biography. It is an interpretive account, rooted in publicly known facts, shared professional memory, and reasoned judgment. Any errors of interpretation are mine alone.

If this book succeeds, it will not be because it celebrates a man, but because it preserves a way of thinking — one that insists that integrity can be designed, excellence can be taught, and leadership can outlast authority.

Subba Rao Chaganti

Preface

This book was written to answer a quiet but persistent question:

How did Indian pharmaceutical marketing learn to think of itself as a profession?

For many years, the industry grew on energy and enterprise. Brands were built, markets expanded, and careers took shape. Yet beneath that progress lay a fragility. Knowledge was personal rather than institutional. Success depended more on individuals than on systems. When people moved on, understanding often moved with them.

What the industry lacked was not ambition or intelligence. It lacked method.

I encountered this gap early in my own career — at a time when I had the privilege of working and learning under Tarun Gupta's tutelage. Those years were formative. They were not marked by inspiration or rhetoric, but by discipline. Thinking was questioned. Assumptions were tested. Execution was scrutinized. Growth, when it came, was earned.

What became clear to me then — and even clearer in hindsight — was that Indian pharmaceutical marketing did not need motivation. It needed teaching. Not teaching as instruction, but teaching as the insistence that experience be converted into systems, and systems into habit.

Tarun Gupta was such a teacher.

Known to generations simply as "TG," he resisted elevation and distrusted slogans. He had little patience for explanations that could not survive the field. What he offered instead was clarity — about roles, responsibility, and the distinction between thinking well and acting well.

This book does not seek to canonize him. Nor is it an authorized biography or a chronological corporate history. It is an interpretive account of how a way of thinking took shape and spread — across companies, classrooms, and generations — without ever being formally owned.

Much of what follows focuses on systems: the Strategy–Execution Quadrant, disciplined field execution, product management as leadership, prescription auditing, training architectures, and integrity designed into process. This emphasis is intentional. TG believed leadership revealed itself not in speeches, but in structures that endured after the leader stepped away.

Equally important are the moments of restraint — decisions not taken, opportunities declined, growth postponed. In an era that celebrates expansion, TG believed judgment was defined as much by what one refused to do as by what one pursued.

This book is written for practitioners, leaders, students, and educators. But above all, it is written for those who believe that industries mature not merely by growing larger, but by learning how to learn.

Indian pharmaceutical marketing reached that moment.

Tarun Gupta helped it cross the threshold.

That is the story this book sets out to tell.

Subba Rao Chaganti

Contents

PART II: THE GLAXO TRANSFORMATION – FROM NUTRITION TO MEDICINE

PART III: THE SCIENCE OF THE "CLINIC" – PROFESSIONALIZING THE FIELD

Part I

The Boots Foundation – Genesis of a Disruptor

Disruption Begins with Discipline

Tarun Gupta did not enter the pharmaceutical industry with the intention of disrupting it. He entered it intending to understand how work was done.

His formative years unfolded under British management, where systems were orderly, expectations explicit, and roles clearly defined. This environment taught him a lasting lesson: discipline is not restrictive—it is enabling. When fundamentals are clear, judgment has room to operate.

At the same time, Gupta became acutely aware of the limits of imported frameworks. Policies designed for distant markets often failed to account for local realities. What worked in theory did not always work in practice. This tension—between structure and context—became the crucible in which his thinking was formed.

Disruption, as Gupta came to practice it, was not rebellion. It was a selective adaptation. He learned which rules to respect, which to reinterpret, and which to discard when they obscured purpose. Authority, for him, was never an excuse for unthinking compliance.

The principle that emerges in this part is foundational:

True disruption does not begin by rejecting systems—it begins by mastering them, and then refining them with judgment.

Part I traces how that discipline was acquired, tested, and quietly transformed into a way of thinking that would later reshape an industry.

Every transformative career has an origin story—not a moment of triumph, but a period of apprenticeship where habits are formed, instincts sharpened, and convictions quietly forged. For Dr. Tarun Gupta, that crucible was Boots, the British pharmaceutical and retail institution whose disciplined systems, understated leadership, and unapologetic pragmatism would leave an indelible mark on a young Indian manager destined to redraw the contours of pharmaceutical marketing in India.

This was not the kind of disruption born of rebellion for its own sake. It was disruption rooted in observation. At Boots, Tarun Gupta encountered something rare in the Indian corporate environment of the time: marketing stripped of theatrics and anchored instead in clarity of thought, operational rigor, and respect for the realities of the field. The British influence he absorbed was not ideological but behavioral—how decisions were made, how accountability was enforced, and how authority could be exercised without bluster.

Central to this formative phase was a mentor who would shape Gupta's managerial DNA in lasting ways: Larry Coombs. Coombs was not a theoretician, nor a believer in grand abstractions. He was, in Gupta's later telling, a "dovish" boss—calm, practical, unflappable—who valued judgment over jargon and outcomes over rhetoric. From him, Gupta learned a lesson that would become foundational to his philosophy: marketing is not what looks good on paper; it is what survives contact with the marketplace.

Yet this British system, for all its elegance, existed in tension with Indian reality. The field force operated in a world shaped by cultural nuance, scarcity, and improvisation—far removed from the neat assumptions of head-office guidelines. It was here, in the friction between "Sahib logic" and Indian ground truth, that Gupta's disruptive instincts were first awakened. He did not reject the system; he adapted it. He did not oppose authority; he translated it.

The incidents that defined this period—some legendary, others quietly consequential—reveal a mind already thinking beyond compliance. Whether it was navigating cultural misunderstandings, questioning rigid margin rules, or taking calculated personal risks to protect a brand's future, Gupta was beginning to articulate a belief that would later revolutionize Indian pharma marketing: systems must serve the market, not the other way around.

Most consequentially, this was the phase in which Gupta discovered the power of repetition, discipline, and long-term investment—ideas that would later crystallize into his iconic "wave-after-wave" philosophy. He saw that brands are not built through sporadic bursts of enthusiasm but through sustained, methodical pressure applied with consistency and respect for the intelligence of the field.

Part I of this book is not merely a historical prologue. It is the intellectual bedrock on which everything that follows stands. The daring decisions at Glaxo, the professionalization of product management, the science of clinic marketing, and the creation of an entire generation of marketing leaders can all be traced back to these early Boots years. Here, the disruptor was not yet a legend—but the contours of his strategic genius were already unmistakably visible.

This is the story of how a young manager learned to see the pharmaceutical business not as a hierarchy to obey, but as a system to be understood, challenged, and—when necessary—reimagined.

Chapter 1

The British Influence and the "Dovish" Boss

Larry Coombs and the Quiet Power of Practicality

Larry Coombs did not teach marketing as a discipline to be admired. He treated it as a craft to be practiced.

His reviews rarely centered on the elegance of thought. Instead, they returned repeatedly to one question: What will change tomorrow morning in the field?

For Tarun Gupta, this was revelatory. It reframed marketing from an intellectual performance into an operational responsibility. The idea that clarity was kindness—and ambiguity a managerial failure—would later resurface in Gupta's own insistence on disciplined detailing, standardized messaging, and repeatable systems.

Long before he became a teacher himself, Gupta had learned the most enduring lesson of his career: marketing that cannot be executed is not strategy—it is decoration.

When Tarun Gupta arrived at Boots, he stepped into a corporate culture that felt almost alien to the Indian pharmaceutical world of the time. This was not an organization driven by flamboyance or charismatic authority. It was quieter than that—measured, deliberate, and almost disarmingly modest. Decisions were made without drama. Success was assumed to result from good systems rather than from heroic individuals. For Gupta, this environment would become a living classroom.

Boots carried the imprint of British managerial tradition at its most refined: an emphasis on order, process, and calm competence. Meetings were purposeful, not performative. Instructions were clear, rarely repeated, and never theatrical. There was an unspoken expectation that once something was decided, it would be executed precisely—without excuses, without improvisation masquerading as creativity. This was Gupta's first sustained exposure to marketing as a discipline rather than a display.

At the center of this experience was Larry Coombs, Gupta's immediate superior and, in many ways, his most consequential early mentor. Coombs did not resemble the commanding, authoritarian bosses common in Indian industry at the time. He was what Gupta would later describe as "dovish"—soft-spoken, patient, and notably unthreatening. Yet this gentleness was deceptive. Coombs was exacting in his expectations and unsentimental in his judgments. He did not raise his voice; he raised standards.

What Coombs offered was not instruction in theory but immersion in practice. He believed that marketing wisdom was situational—that it emerged from close engagement with the field rather than from academic abstraction. Data mattered, but context mattered more. Reports were useful only if they led to action. In review meetings, Coombs had a way of listening longer than he spoke, asking a single question that cut through pages of explanation and revealed whether the presenter truly understood the problem.

From Coombs, Gupta absorbed a principle that would guide him throughout his career: clarity is kindness. Ambiguity, in Coombs' world, was a managerial failure. If a sales representative misunderstood an objective, the fault lay not with the representative but with the system that failed to make the objective unmistakable. This belief would later inform Gupta's obsession with simple, repeatable detailing messages and his intolerance for decorative but useless promotional material.

Yet the British influence was not without its blind spots. The assumptions embedded in Boots' policies—about margins, market behavior, and field discipline—were rooted in a European context far removed from Indian realities. Gupta saw this early. He observed how well-intentioned guidelines could collapse when confronted with shortages, fragmented trade channels, and deeply hierarchical social norms. The system was elegant, but the terrain was unforgiving.

One incident, later remembered in the organization as the "Ghungroo" episode, crystallized this cultural gap. A seemingly minor misunderstanding—born of language, symbolism, and unspoken hierarchy—exposed the distance between British managerial intent and Indian lived experience. Gupta found himself navigating not just a professional dilemma but a cultural one, mediating between the expectations of the "Sahibs" and the sensibilities of Indian managers and field staff. It was here that he learned a subtle but powerful lesson: authority in India is not merely assigned; it is interpreted.

Rather than dismissing the British system, Gupta began to internalize it selectively. He admired its discipline but rejected its rigidity. He respected its insistence on accountability but recognized the need for contextual flexibility. This synthesis—British structure fused with Indian realism—would become the hallmark of his later work.

By the end of his Boots years, Gupta had undergone a quiet transformation. He had learned that effective leadership did not require intimidation, that marketing excellence depended more on execution than eloquence, and that systems, when thoughtfully adapted, could scale human judgment rather than replace it.

Larry Coombs may have been dovish in temperament, but the lessons he imparted were sharp and enduring. In absorbing them, Tarun Gupta was not merely being trained. He was being prepared for a career that would challenge orthodoxy, professionalize an industry, and teach an entire generation of Indian pharmaceutical marketers how to think.

Learning from Larry Coombs: Practicality over Academia

Larry Coombs did not teach in classrooms, and he did not quote textbooks. His lessons were delivered in corridors, review meetings, and long, unhurried conversations that began with simple questions and ended with quiet clarity. For Tarun Gupta, this was an education unlike any he had encountered—one that treated management not as a body of knowledge to be mastered, but as a craft to be practiced.

Coombs had little patience for academic grandstanding. He was not dismissive of theory, but he was wary of it when it arrived unaccompanied by judgment. In his world, an elegant framework was meaningless unless it could survive the messiness of real markets. He often asked a deceptively simple question after presentations dense with analysis: What will the representative do differently tomorrow morning? If the answer was unclear, the work was unfinished.

This insistence on applicability left a deep impression on Gupta. He began to see how easily managers could hide behind jargon, mistaking complexity for insight. Coombs had an instinctive ability to strip a problem down to its essentials. He was less interested in why something should work and more focused on whether it did. Evidence, for him, was not statistical elegance but behavioral change in the field.

Coombs also believed that the best ideas rarely emerged from head office. He encouraged Gupta to spend time observing sales representatives—not to inspect them, but to understand them. He treated the field not as an execution arm but as a sensing organ, capable of revealing truths that never appeared in reports. Marketing, in this view, was not persuasion conceived in isolation; it was problem-solving conducted in dialogue with reality.

One of Coombs' most enduring influences was his approach to decision-making under uncertainty. He accepted that information would always be incomplete, especially in emerging markets. Waiting for perfect data, he believed, was simply another form of indecision. Instead, he emphasized disciplined experimentation—act, observe, adjust. Mistakes were tolerated if they were honest and instructive; indecision was not.

For Gupta, this was liberating. It reframed risk not as something to be avoided but as something to be managed intelligently. The courage to act, anchored in practical reasoning, became a defining feature of his later career. Whether challenging margin rules, investing in brands before they were profitable, or enforcing detailing discipline, Gupta would repeatedly echo Coombs' philosophy: action, when thoughtfully designed, teaches more than theory ever could.

Perhaps most importantly, Coombs modeled a quiet confidence that came from mastery rather than authority. He did not need to assert his expertise; it was evident in the way he listened, questioned, and decided. This demeanor showed Gupta that leadership credibility is earned through consistency of judgment, not through titles or rhetoric.

In learning from Larry Coombs, Tarun Gupta absorbed a worldview that would later place him at odds with much of conventional marketing education. He came to believe that textbooks should follow practice, not precede it; that frameworks are useful only when born of experience; and that the true test of marketing intelligence is not how well one can explain an idea, but how effectively one can make it work.

This preference for practicality over academia would later define Gupta as both a corporate leader and a teacher. Long before he challenged students in Indian classrooms to value practice over theory, he had learned that lesson firsthand—quietly, decisively, from a dovish boss who taught by example rather than instruction.

The "Ghungroo" Incident

Navigating the Cultural Divide Between the "Sahibs" and Indian Managers

The incident itself was, on the surface, trivial. A word. A gesture. An object whose meaning shifted depending on who was looking at it. Yet in retrospect, the "Ghungroo" episode would come to symbolize something far larger—the invisible fault line between British managerial intent and Indian cultural reality, and the quiet skill with which Tarun Gupta learned to walk that line.

In the British managerial lexicon at Boots, symbols were assumed to be neutral. A token could be motivational, a gesture merely symbolic, or an instruction purely functional. But India did not operate on neutral symbols. Here, meaning was layered, hierarchical, and deeply contextual. What was benign in Nottingham could feel patronizing in Nagpur. What was light-hearted to a "Sahib" could be humiliating to an Indian manager who carried centuries of cultural memory into every professional interaction.

The "Ghungroo"—a small anklet bell associated in India with dancers, performers, and, in some contexts, social subordination—entered the corporate space with no malice attached to it. To the British leadership, it was an innocuous prop, perhaps even a playful metaphor. To Indian managers and field staff, it carried connotations that could not be spoken aloud in a colonial corporate hierarchy but were felt instantly and viscerally.

When discomfort surfaced, it did so indirectly. There was no open protest, no confrontation. Instead, Gupta sensed a shift in energy—hesitation, lowered eyes, strained politeness. This was the India he knew well: dissent expressed through silence, resistance communicated through compliance. The British managers, accustomed to explicit feedback, missed the signal entirely.

Gupta found himself in an unenviable position. He was young, ambitious, and operating within a British system that valued clarity and directness. Yet he also understood the unspoken codes governing Indian professional dignity. To challenge the "Sahibs" directly would risk being seen as oversensitive or insubordinate. To ignore the issue would erode trust among Indian colleagues who were watching closely to see whether one of their own would recognize the insult embedded in the gesture.

What Gupta did next revealed a nascent leadership instinct that would later define his career. He did not frame the issue as a cultural offense. Instead, he translated it into managerial effectiveness. He explained—calmly, factually—that symbols operate differently across cultures, and that unintended humiliation could quietly undermine morale, execution, and respect for authority. The argument was not emotional; it was operational.

This reframing made all the difference. The British managers listened—not because they were being accused, but because they were being informed. The "Ghungroo" was withdrawn without drama, apology, or escalation. The system adjusted. Dignity was restored. No one lost face.

For Gupta, the episode became a formative lesson in cross-cultural leadership. He learned that authority does not require confrontation, and that change is often best achieved through translation rather than opposition. The role of a leader in such contexts, he realized, is not to amplify conflict but to convert it into understanding.

More subtly, the incident taught him that systems imported from elsewhere must be interpreted locally if they are to function at all. Respect, in India, was not a soft value—it was an operational necessity. A demotivated representative might still show up for work, but he would not bring judgment, initiative, or pride to the task.

Years later, when Gupta would design training programs, selection systems, and incentive structures, the memory of the "Ghungroo" incident lingered. He would become acutely sensitive to how messages landed, how authority was experienced, and how easily well-meaning policies could alienate the very people they were meant to inspire.

The "Ghungroo" episode never appeared in official reports. It did not alter a balance sheet or change a product strategy. Yet it quietly shaped a philosophy: that great management lies in understanding not just what is said, but what is felt; not just what is intended, but what is interpreted.

In navigating that moment, Tarun Gupta was doing more than resolving a misunderstanding. He was learning how to bridge worlds—a skill that would later allow him to bring global marketing discipline into India without erasing Indian identity.

Chapter 2

The Sweetex Gamble: Defying International Policy

"You Can't Run Marketing by Remote Control"

When questioned by international leadership for violating pricing protocol during the sugar shortage, Tarun Gupta did not plead circumstance.

His response was blunt: Either you take all the decisions—or I do.

It was not defiance. It was accountability.

The remark captured a philosophy that would later define his leadership style: global systems may guide, but local managers must decide. Markets do not respond to headquarters—they respond to availability, relevance, and trust.

Every system, no matter how well designed, eventually encounters a moment when obedience and judgment collide. For Tarun Gupta, that moment arrived with Sweetex—a product that, under ordinary circumstances, should have followed a carefully prescribed international playbook. Instead, it became the stage on which he made one of his earliest and most consequential decisions: to place local reality above global doctrine.

At the time, Boots operated under a rigid international margin policy. The rule was clear, elegant, and non-negotiable on paper: a minimum of sixty percent gross margin was mandatory for any product the company sold. The policy made perfect sense in stable, mature markets where supply chains were predictable and pricing power was assured. India, however, was neither stable nor mature. It was a market shaped by shortages, rationing, and abrupt shifts in availability—conditions under which rules designed for Europe began to fray.

Sweetex entered this environment at precisely the wrong time. Sugar was in short supply, and when sugar becomes scarce in India, it ceases to be a commodity and becomes a political and emotional substance. Prices fluctuated wildly. Availability was erratic. Yet demand for a sugar substitute did not vanish; if anything, it intensified. For Gupta, this created a dilemma that no policy manual could resolve.

By strict international standards, Sweetex should have been deprioritized or withdrawn. Maintaining the mandated margin under local conditions would have required pricing the product out of reach for most consumers. The policy was logical—but the outcome would have been commercial irrelevance. Gupta saw this immediately. A brand, he understood, does not live on spreadsheets. It lives in kitchens, shops, and daily habits.

The decision he faced was stark. He could comply with policy and protect his position, or he could bend the rule and give the brand a chance to survive. Choosing the latter meant violating a clearly articulated international directive. It also meant something far more personal: risking his career.

Gupta chose the market.

He argued that margins are not moral absolutes; they are strategic variables. In a crisis, he believed, relevance mattered more than percentage points. He proposed a pricing and margin structure that fell short of the international benchmark but allowed Sweetex to remain accessible during the sugar shortage. The logic was simple and deeply practical: Sugar is short. Sweetex should not be.

This was not defiance for its own sake. It was a calculated, evidence-based bet that long-term brand equity would outweigh short-term margin dilution. Gupta was betting not just on the product, but on the intelligence of consumers and the resilience of demand. If Sweetex disappeared when it was most needed, the brand would not be forgiven when conditions normalized.

The risk, however, was very real. International headquarters did not reward contextual innovation. Deviations from policy were treated as breaches, not experiments. Gupta was fully aware that the “chopper”—as termination was colloquially known—hung visibly over decisions like this. Yet he proceeded with a calm that reflected a deeper conviction: that leadership meant absorbing risk so the system could learn.

The outcome vindicated the judgment. Sweetex remained present, affordable, and relevant during the crisis. When sugar supplies stabilized, the brand emerged stronger, with loyalty built not through promotion but through reliability. Consumers remembered who stayed when it mattered.

More importantly, the episode clarified something fundamental in Gupta's thinking. He began to see global policy not as a commandment, but as a hypothesis—valid until reality proved otherwise. Markets, he concluded, do not reward obedience; they reward understanding.

The Sweetex gamble marked a turning point. It signaled the emergence of a manager willing to reinterpret rules in service of outcomes, and to defend those interpretations with reason rather than rebellion. It also foreshadowed the philosophy that would later define his legacy: that marketing excellence lies in the courage to choose relevance over rigidity, even when the personal cost is high.

This was not yet the Tarun Gupta who would professionalize Indian pharmaceutical marketing. But in choosing the market over the manual, he took a decisive step toward becoming that man.

Challenging the 60% Margin Rule

Choosing Local Opportunity over British Guidelines

Rules, Larry Coombs often reminded his team, exist to reduce error—not to eliminate judgment. Yet some rules, once institutionalized, acquire a moral authority of their own. At Boots, the sixty percent margin requirement had become such a rule. It was not merely a financial guideline; it was a proxy for managerial discipline, a signal that the company would not dilute its standards in the face of local pressure. In theory, it ensured consistency. In practice, in India, it threatened relevance.

For Tarun Gupta, the rule presented itself not as an abstract policy but as a lived contradiction. The Indian market of the time was fragmented, volatile, and intensely price-sensitive. Distribution was uneven. Consumer purchasing power fluctuated. And during periods of scarcity—particularly the sugar shortages that framed the Sweetex episode—price ceased to be a lever and became a barrier. A product that could not be bought might as well not exist.

Gupta approached the problem not as a rebel but as a diagnostician. He asked a question that few dared to articulate: What is the purpose of the margin rule? If the objective was to protect brand health and ensure sustainable profitability, then blindly enforcing it in a distorted market achieved the opposite. High margins on negligible volumes were not a triumph of discipline; they were an abdication of responsibility.

British guidelines assumed a stable equilibrium—predictable input costs, consistent consumer demand, and orderly trade behavior. India offered none of these. Gupta saw that applying the rule without interpretation would force Sweetex into a niche so narrow that it would lose both scale and meaning. The brand would survive on paper, but vanish in practice.

The alternative was uncomfortable. Reducing margins meant inviting scrutiny from headquarters, where deviation was often conflated with incompetence. Gupta knew that the decision would be read not in context, but against a spreadsheet. Yet he also knew something more important: brands are built in moments of stress, not stability.

He framed his argument carefully. This was not about lowering standards; it was about sequencing them. Margin optimization, he contended, was a second-order problem. First came availability. Then came trust. Profitability would follow—not instantly, but inevitably—if the brand remained present when consumers needed it most. To insist on sixty percent margins in the midst of a shortage was, in effect, to abandon the market to competitors willing to adapt.

What distinguished Gupta's challenge was its tone. He did not accuse the British system of being wrong; he demonstrated where it was incomplete. He showed how local opportunity, if seized intelligently, could strengthen the very principles the guidelines sought to protect. This was not defiance; it was translation.

The decision to prioritize local opportunity required a quiet kind of courage. There were no public victories, no immediate accolades. The risk was asymmetrical: if the gamble failed, Gupta would bear the consequences alone; if it succeeded, the system would absorb the credit. He accepted this imbalance without complaint.

In doing so, he crystallized a belief that would later shape his entire philosophy of marketing leadership: that rules are instruments, not idols; that global wisdom must bow to local truth; and that managerial maturity lies in knowing when to comply and when to reinterpret.

Challenging the sixty percent margin rule was not a dramatic confrontation. It was a measured, reasoned, and deeply practical act of leadership. And in that choice—to stand with the market rather than the manual—Tarun Gupta signaled the emergence of a strategist who understood that the ultimate loyalty of a marketer must be not to policy, but to relevance.

Sugar is Short. Sweetex is Not

Agility in a Crisis

Crises have a way of clarifying what organizations truly value. When sugar supplies tightened across India, uncertainty spread quickly—not just through households and kirana stores, but through boardrooms and planning documents. For many companies, the instinctive response was retreat: reduce exposure, conserve margins, wait for stability to return. Tarun Gupta chose a different response. He chose presence.

The phrase that came to define the moment—"Sugar is short. Sweetex is not."—was not conceived as a slogan. It was a strategic stance, compressed into six words. It reflected an understanding that when a staple disappears, the substitute must not. Scarcity, Gupta believed, was not a reason to withdraw; it was a call to act with speed, clarity, and moral confidence.

What made the crisis particularly treacherous was its unpredictability. Supply disruptions cascaded without warning. Prices swung sharply. Distribution networks strained under pressure. In such conditions, rigid planning became a liability. Gupta responded by privileging agility over optimization. He accepted thinner margins, reworked supply assumptions, and pushed the organization to prioritize continuity over perfection.

This was not improvisation masquerading as strategy. It was disciplined flexibility. Gupta insisted on rapid feedback from the field—daily signals from distributors, pharmacists, and sales representatives. Decisions were revisited frequently, not to second-guess them, but to refine them. The objective was simple and unwavering: Sweetex must remain available wherever demand existed.

In doing so, Gupta reframed the crisis as an opportunity for trust-building. Consumers do not remember quarterly margins; they remember who stood by them when options disappeared. By ensuring that Sweetex did not vanish during a sugar shortage, the brand became more than a product. It became a reliable presence in a moment of disruption.

There was also a psychological dimension to the decision. Internally, it signaled that leadership was willing to absorb risk on behalf of the organization. Externally, it conveyed confidence. A brand that stays visible during a crisis communicates stability—even when the environment is unstable. Gupta understood that visibility, in such moments, is itself a form of reassurance.

The cost of this approach was immediate and measurable. Margins compressed. Questions from headquarters intensified. The specter of reprimand—or worse—was never far away. Yet Gupta did not flinch. He believed that retreat would be remembered far longer than any temporary financial sacrifice.

When sugar supplies eventually normalized, Sweetex emerged not weakened but strengthened. Distribution relationships had deepened. Consumer loyalty had hardened into habit. The brand had passed a stress test that no advertising campaign could have engineered.

Looking back, the episode revealed something essential about Gupta's strategic temperament. He was not enamored with crisis rhetoric, nor did he romanticize risk. His agility was rooted in preparation, observation, and respect for reality. He moved quickly because he understood the system deeply.

"Sugar is short. Sweetex is not." endures not because it was clever, but because it was true. It captured a philosophy that would later define Gupta's approach to marketing and leadership: that in moments of scarcity, the most valuable asset a brand can offer is not price or promotion, but presence.

Facing the Chopper

The Risk of Personal Termination for the Sake of Brand Success

In multinational organizations, discipline is often enforced not through confrontation, but through consequence. There is no raised voice, no public reprimand—only a quiet finality. At Boots, the euphemism for this was the "chopper." It did not descend often, but its presence was understood by everyone. Deviate too far from policy, and the system would correct itself—by removing you.

Tarun Gupta knew this. He knew it when he questioned the sixty percent margin rule. He knew it when he chose availability over compliance during the sugar shortage. And he knew it most acutely as Sweetex continued to operate outside the boundaries of international guidelines. Every decision carried a subtext: Is this worth my job?

What made the risk unusually stark was the absence of ambiguity. The rules had been written. The deviations were visible. There was no plausible deniability. Gupta was not experimenting in the shadows; he was making choices in full view of a system that prized uniformity. The possibility of termination was not dramatic—it was procedural.

Yet Gupta did not treat the risk theatrically. He neither sought martyrdom nor attempted to justify himself preemptively. His posture was pragmatic, almost clinical. He believed that if the decision was right for the brand and right for the market, it was defensible—even if it proved personally costly.

This mindset marked a departure from the managerial norm of the time, where career preservation often outweighed strategic conviction. Gupta inverted the equation. He reasoned that a manager who protects his position at the expense of the business is already compromised. If leadership did not involve absorbing risk, then it was merely administration.

There was also an ethical dimension to the choice. Pulling Sweetex back during a shortage would have been easier—and safer. But it would have betrayed the trust of distributors, retailers, and consumers who had come to rely on the product. Gupta understood that brands are social contracts, not just financial assets. To abandon the market in a moment of need would fracture that contract.

Facing the chopper, then, became less about fear and more about clarity. Gupta accepted that outcomes are uncertain, but intent matters. He did not believe that loyalty reminded headquarters of policy; he believed it reminded them of purpose. If the system could not recognize that distinction, the failure would not be his alone.

The chopper never fell. But that was almost incidental. What mattered more was the precedent the episode set—for Gupta and for those who observed him closely. It established a standard of leadership that prioritized responsibility over security, judgment over obedience, and long-term brand health over short-term personal comfort.

Years later, when Gupta would insist that brand managers think like owners and accept accountability beyond their job descriptions, the memory of Sweetex lingered. He had learned, early on, that meaningful impact often reminded systems of their own rigidity—and that progress sometimes requires standing calmly beneath the blade.

Facing the chopper was not an act of defiance. It was an act of alignment—with the market, with the brand, and with a personal code that would guide Tarun Gupta throughout a career defined not by safety, but by significance.

Chapter 3

The Birth of the "Wave-after-Wave" Campaign

Why Repetition Works (When It Usually Doesn't)

Most brands fail not because their messages are wrong, but because they change them too soon.

Gupta understood something counterintuitive: repetition does not bore when it creates familiarity. It bores only when it lacks meaning.

The "wave-after-wave" philosophy treated promotion as cumulative learning—not persuasion by force, but understanding by exposure. It demanded patience, consistency, and the courage to resist novelty for its own sake.

Most marketing failures, Tarun Gupta observed early in his career, did not stem from poor ideas. They stemmed from impatience. Brands were launched with enthusiasm, promoted in bursts, and abandoned just as familiarity began to take root. The assumption—rarely questioned—was that impact came from novelty. At Boots, and later through his own experiments, Gupta arrived at a very different conclusion: impact comes from repetition, intelligently applied.

The "wave-after-wave" campaign was not born in a boardroom. It emerged from a growing dissatisfaction with sporadic promotion—the start-stop rhythm that characterized much of pharmaceutical marketing at the time. Sales representatives were sent into the field with messages that changed too often, visual aids that dazzled briefly and then disappeared, and targets that assumed awareness could be created on demand. Gupta saw the flaw immediately. Doctors, like all human beings, do not reorganize their thinking with each new visit. They absorb meaning slowly, through accumulation.

What Gupta proposed was deceptively simple. Instead of treating each campaign as a standalone event, he would treat it as part of a sequence. Each wave would reinforce the previous one. The message would remain stable, the core promise unmistakable, while execution improved incrementally with each cycle. Promotion, in this model, was not a burst—it was a current.

This required a fundamental shift in mindset. Management had to abandon the illusion that marketing was a creative sprint and accept that it was an endurance discipline. Sales teams had to resist the temptation to "refresh" messages prematurely. And perhaps most difficult of all, senior leadership had to invest without demanding immediate returns.

The launch of Digene Gel became the proving ground for this philosophy. Rather than flooding the market and waiting for instant traction, Gupta structured the campaign to build presence methodically. Detailing was standardized. Frequency was non-negotiable. Every interaction was designed to sound familiar, not novel. Over time, the message did not merely register—it settled.

Gupta understood something that data would later confirm: familiarity breeds trust, not contempt, when it is earned rather than imposed. Doctors began to anticipate the message. Representatives gained confidence through mastery rather than improvisation. The brand, once obscure, acquired a steady, almost gravitational pull in the market.

The "wave-after-wave" approach also reflected a deeper investment philosophy. Gupta rejected the notion that brands must break even in their first year to be considered successful. Early profitability, he believed, was often a sign of under-investment. True brands required time—time to educate, time to embed habits, time to become part of a professional routine. He was willing to trade short-term financial comfort for long-term strategic dominance.

This philosophy ran counter to prevailing norms. Many organizations treated marketing budgets as experiments to be judged quickly and cut ruthlessly. Gupta treated them as commitments. Once a wave began, it was not withdrawn mid-stream. Consistency, he believed, was a form of respect—for the field force, for the customer, and for the brand itself.

The birth of the "wave-after-wave" campaign marked a turning point in Gupta's thinking. It transformed marketing from an act of persuasion into a system of belief-building. It also laid the groundwork for practices that would later professionalize the industry: disciplined detailing, message control, and the elevation of repetition from a tactical necessity to a strategic virtue.

In retrospect, the idea seems obvious. At the time, it was quietly radical. By choosing persistence over novelty and systems over spectacle, Tarun Gupta was not just launching a campaign. He was redefining how pharmaceutical brands would be built in India—one wave at a time.

Launching Digene Gel

Moving from Sporadic Promotion to Systematic, Repetitive Impact

When Digene Gel was ready to enter the market, it faced a challenge that had little to do with formulation and everything to do with attention. The antacid category was crowded, noisy, and accustomed to short bursts of promotion that flared brightly and then faded. Most brands announced themselves loudly, spent heavily, and waited—often in vain—for prescriptions to follow. Tarun Gupta saw in Digene Gel not just a product to be launched, but an opportunity to challenge this deeply ingrained pattern.

The prevailing model of promotion was episodic. Campaigns were conceived as events rather than processes. Messages changed with managerial enthusiasm, not market absorption. Sales representatives were asked to be inventive rather than consistent. Gupta recognized that this approach confused novelty with progress. Doctors, overwhelmed by competing claims, learned to tune out what did not persist.

Gupta chose a different path. He treated the Digene Gel launch as a long conversation rather than a dramatic announcement. The objective was not immediate recall, but gradual imprinting. From the outset, the message was kept deliberately simple and stable. It would not be refreshed until it had been understood, internalized, and remembered.

This required discipline at every level of the organization. Sales representatives were trained not to embellish, not to improvise, and not to chase approval through cleverness. Mastery replaced novelty. Repetition replaced rhetoric. Each call reinforced the same core idea, delivered with increasing confidence and precision.

What made the approach radical was its refusal to equate activity with effectiveness. Gupta did not measure success by the number of promotional materials distributed or slogans introduced. He measured it by consistency of execution. A representative who delivered the same message accurately, week after week, was doing superior work—even if nothing about it appeared exciting.

Over time, something subtle but powerful occurred. Doctors began to recognize the Digene Gel narrative before it was completed. Familiarity replaced skepticism. The brand's presence became predictable, and in that predictability lay trust. Digene Gel was no longer just another antacid; it was a known quantity.

Gupta understood that repetition, when intelligently designed, reduces cognitive effort. Doctors did not need to re-evaluate the brand at every visit. The mental energy saved translated into openness. Prescriptions followed not because the message was new, but because it was settled.

Equally important was the organizational impact. Sales teams gained confidence from clarity. They knew exactly what success looked like. Performance variation narrowed—not because everyone became exceptional, but because everyone became competent. Gupta was building not just a brand, but a system.

The Digene Gel launch validated a conviction that would later define Gupta's legacy: that sustainable impact in pharmaceutical marketing is rarely the result of brilliance in isolation. It is the outcome of persistence, structure, and respect for how human attention actually works.

By moving from sporadic promotion to systematic, repetitive impact, Gupta did more than launch a successful product. He demonstrated that marketing, at its best, is not a series of clever moments—but a discipline of continuity.

Vignette: The Imposition

Detailing Perfection, Written Twenty-Five Times

The instruction, when it came, sounded almost punitive.

Sales representatives were told to write the Digene Gel story—word for word—twenty-five times. By hand. No shortcuts. No paraphrasing. No creative liberties. For a field force accustomed to verbal persuasion and visual aids, the task felt archaic, even humiliating. Murmurs followed. Some wondered whether this was discipline masquerading as punishment. Others suspected it was a test of endurance rather than intelligence.

Tarun Gupta listened, but he did not waver.

To understand the imposition, one had to understand Gupta's growing unease with how detailing was practiced. Representatives spoke fluently, sometimes brilliantly, but with alarming inconsistency. Messages drifted. Emphasis shifted. What reached the doctor depended less on strategy and more on individual interpretation. In a "wave-after-wave" system, such variability was fatal. Repetition required precision; precision required internalization.

Gupta believed that before a message could be delivered persuasively, it had to be possessed completely. Writing, he knew, forces confrontation with one's own vagueness. The hand exposes what the mouth can conceal. By repeatedly writing the Digene Gel story, representatives were not memorizing text—they were embedding structure.

The exercise was exhausting by design. The first few iterations were mechanical. By the tenth, irritation set in. Somewhere around the fifteenth, something shifted. Words that had once felt imposed began to feel familiar. The sequence stabilized. The logic revealed itself. By the twenty-fifth, the story no longer belonged to the page. It belonged to the representative.

This was not an act of authoritarian control. It was a method. Gupta was imposing discipline not to restrict expression, but to liberate it from error. Once the structure was internalized, delivery became effortless. Confidence replaced improvisation. Silence between sentences grew comfortable rather than awkward.

The effect in the field was immediate and striking. Detailing became crisp, consistent, and unmistakably aligned. Doctors heard the same story regardless of who called on them or where. The brand's message no longer wavered with personality. It arrived intact.

What made the vignette legendary was not the exercise itself, but what it revealed about Gupta's philosophy. He was willing to cause short-term discomfort to eliminate confusion in the long term. He understood that freedom without mastery is noise, and that standardization, when thoughtfully applied, is not the enemy of intelligence.

Years later, many of those representatives would recall the exercise with reluctant admiration. What had once felt excessive revealed itself as formative. They had learned, perhaps for the first time, what excellence in execution actually required.

"The Imposition," as it came to be known, captured the essence of Tarun Gupta's approach: demanding, exacting, and quietly respectful of the craft. In insisting that the Digene Gel story be written twenty-five times, he was not enforcing obedience. He was teaching a generation of marketers that precision is not optional—and that mastery begins where repetition ends.

The Investment Philosophy

Why Brands should not be Forced to Break Even in Year One?

In many organizations, the first year of a brand's life is treated as a trial. Budgets are released cautiously, expectations are framed in financial terms, and success is measured by a single, unforgiving metric: break-even. For Tarun Gupta, this approach betrayed a fundamental misunderstanding of how brands are built—and why most of them fail.

Gupta had come to see brands not as products with promotional support, but as long-term assets that require deliberate nurturing. Expecting a brand to recover its investment in the first year, he believed, was akin to demanding a return before trust had time to form. Awareness could be bought quickly. Acceptance could not.

The insistence on year-one profitability, Gupta argued, created perverse incentives. Managers cut back on frequency, dilute messaging, and withdraw support at the first sign of resistance. Campaigns are shortened just as familiarity begins to develop. In the process, brands are denied the very conditions they need to succeed. What appears prudent on a balance sheet becomes destructive in the market.

Drawing from his experience with Digene Gel and earlier lessons at Boots, Gupta reframed the question. Instead of asking when a brand would break even, he asked whether it was becoming known, trusted, and remembered. These were not soft measures; they were leading indicators of future profitability. A brand that achieved them consistently would, in time, justify its investment many times over.

Gupta believed that the early years of a brand's life should be treated as a period of capital formation. Investment during this phase was not a cost to be minimized but a commitment to be honored. Frequency had to be maintained. The "wave-after-wave" discipline had to be protected. Pulling back too early, he warned, did not save money—it squandered it.

This philosophy ran counter to the prevailing culture of quick wins and short reporting cycles. It required patience from leadership and courage from brand managers. It also required a willingness to tolerate ambiguity. Returns would not be immediate. Progress would often go unnoticed by those scanning monthly statements.

Yet Gupta was unsentimental about this patience. He did not advocate indiscriminate spending. Investment, in his view, had to be disciplined, focused, and relentlessly aligned to a clear strategy. What he rejected was the illusion that restraint alone produced efficiency. Under-investment, he argued, was far more expensive than over-investment when measured across a brand's lifetime.

By refusing to force brands to break even in year one, Gupta was asserting a deeper principle: that markets reward consistency, not caution. Brands earn their place gradually, through repeated exposure and reliable performance. To deny them the time required to do so was not conservative—it was shortsighted.

This investment philosophy would later become a cornerstone of Gupta's teaching and practice. He urged marketers to think like stewards rather than accountants, to defend early investment as an act of strategic faith rather than financial recklessness.

In insisting that brands be given time to breathe, Tarun Gupta was not lowering standards. He was raising them—by aligning financial expectations with the realities of human attention, habit, and trust.

Part II

The Glaxo Transformation – From Nutrition to Medicine

How the Industry Later Remembered the Glaxo Years

Decades later, industry observers would describe Tarun Gupta's Glaxo tenure as nothing less than transformational—crediting him with professionalizing pharmaceutical marketing in India and building a generation of leaders fluent in modern marketing principles.

What appeared, at the time, as internal restructuring would later be recognized as the birth of modern pharma marketing in India—a shift from intuition to systems, from promotion to strategy, and from hierarchy to accountability.

If the years at Boots forged Tarun Gupta's instincts, Glaxo gave him scale. What had been learned through observation and selective defiance would now be tested in an organization large enough to amplify ideas—and rigid enough to resist them. This was no longer about adapting a system. It was about transforming one.

When Gupta entered Glaxo, the company stood at a strategic crossroads. Its identity in India was anchored in nutrition—trusted, domestic, almost familial. Products like Complan and Farex had secured a place in households, not clinics. Doctors respected the brand, but they did not yet rely on it. Glaxo was admired, but it was not indispensable. The future lay in medicine, and the path forward was neither obvious nor easy.

Gupta recognized that this shift would require more than portfolio expansion. It demanded a reorientation of mindset. Nutrition brands thrive on reassurance and habit; pharmaceutical brands demand authority and evidence. The competencies that built household familiarity were not sufficient to command clinical trust. To move from nutrition to medicine, Glaxo would have to learn how to think—and act—like a scientific institution, not merely a consumer one.

This transformation unfolded under pressure. Market dynamics were changing rapidly. Competition intensified. Global expectations sharpened. Internally, structures designed for stability struggled to accommodate ambition. Gupta stepped into this environment not as a caretaker but as an architect.

What distinguished his approach was its systemic nature. He did not isolate marketing from sales, or strategy from execution. Instead, he treated the organization as an integrated mechanism, in which clarity at the top had to translate into discipline in the field. Product management would need to be redefined. Planning would need to become intentional rather than reactive. Execution would need to be measured, not assumed.

The Glaxo years would become the laboratory in which Gupta's ideas matured into doctrine. Here, he would articulate the product manager's role as a "mini-CEO." He would dismantle legacy power structures that blurred accountability. He would insist on training not as an event, but as a continuous process. And he would bring data, creativity, and field insight into a single, coherent system.

This was not a transformation through slogans or rebranding. It was a transformation through structure—through the quiet, relentless alignment of people, processes, and purpose. Resistance was inevitable. So were moments of doubt. Yet Gupta pressed forward with the same conviction that had guided him at Boots: that organizations, like brands, change only when repetition replaces rhetoric.

Part II traces this pivotal chapter in Gupta's career, where influence gave way to authority, and ideas found institutional expression. It is the story of how Glaxo, under his strategic guidance, began its evolution from a nutrition-led enterprise into a medicine-driven powerhouse—and how, in doing so, Indian pharmaceutical marketing took a decisive step toward professionalism.

This is where Tarun Gupta stopped adapting systems—and began creating them.

Chapter 4

The Family Products Success – Building Complan and Farex

From Products to Categories

When Tarun Gupta took charge of Glaxo's Family Products Division, his task was not to sell more Complan or Farex. It was to define what these products stood for—and to ensure that every function behaved accordingly.

He believed that strong brands were not created by promotion alone, but by category clarity. Complan was positioned not merely as a nutritional supplement, but as a solution to parental anxiety about growth. Farex was framed not as baby food, but as an entry point into responsible infant nutrition.

This distinction mattered.

Products compete. Categories endure.

By anchoring brands to categories rather than campaigns, TG ensured that marketing, sales, training, and communication moved in the same direction. Execution became easier because thinking was clearer.

The lesson was simple but enduring:

When a brand owns a category, promotion becomes reinforcement—not persuasion.

When Tarun Gupta took charge of Glaxo's Family Products Division, he inherited brands that were familiar but under-leveraged. Complan and Farex were present in Indian households, yet their meanings were diffuse—respected but not sharply defined. They were products people bought, not brands people believed in. Gupta understood that this distinction mattered. Familiarity could sustain volume, but only belief could create leadership.

The strategic challenge was subtle. These were not failing brands in need of rescue. They were comfortable brands in danger of stagnation. In an India where nutrition was often equated with tradition rather than science, Gupta saw an opportunity to elevate the conversation. He believed that if Complan and Farex were to move from pantry staples to category leaders, they would need a clear, defensible reason to exist—one grounded in modern nutritional understanding rather than inherited habit.

Gupta approached the task as a marketer, not a caretaker. His first move was to impose clarity. Each brand would stand for something precise, not everything vaguely. Complan would no longer be just a health drink; it would become a scientifically articulated nutritional supplement. Farex would not merely be baby food; it would position itself as a measured, trustworthy introduction to structured nutrition at a critical developmental stage.

This repositioning demanded courage. Gupta chose to speak directly to the Indian consumer's evolving aspirations—education, upward mobility, and scientific legitimacy. Complan's relaunch was built on a simple but disarming comparison: Your body needs twenty-three vital nutrients. Milk has nine. Complan has all twenty-three. The message was not poetic, but it was unarguable. It reframed nutrition as adequacy rather than abundance.

What distinguished Gupta's execution was its respect for intelligence. He did not rely on emotional excess or exaggerated claims. He trusted that consumers, when presented with a clear rationale, would respond in a rational way. Advertising became a vehicle for explanation rather than persuasion. The brand's voice was confident, not coaxing.

Farex followed a parallel path. Gupta recognized that mothers, more than anyone else, valued reassurance backed by evidence. Farex was positioned not as a convenience, but as a considered choice—one that aligned with pediatric guidance and nutritional completeness. The brand's credibility was reinforced through consistency, frequency, and disciplined messaging.

Behind the scenes, Gupta applied the same systems thinking that had shaped his earlier successes. Marketing plans were integrated with sales execution. Field forces were trained to understand the why behind the message, not merely the what. Budgets were defended as investments, not expenditures. The "wave-after-wave" philosophy ensured that repositioning was not announced and abandoned, but reinforced until it settled into public consciousness.

The results were swift and unmistakable. Complan and Farex did not merely grow; they assumed leadership roles. They became reference points in their categories, benchmarks against which competitors were measured. More importantly, they demonstrated that Indian consumers were ready for scientifically framed marketing—if it was delivered with clarity and respect.

For Gupta, the success of the Family Products Division was more than a commercial victory. It validated a conviction that would guide his later work: that marketing excellence lies not in spectacle, but in structure; not in cleverness, but in coherence. By building Complan and Farex into category leaders, he showed that brands rooted in science, executed with discipline, and sustained through consistency could shape not just markets, but mindsets.

This chapter marks the moment when Gupta moved from promising innovator to proven transformer. The lessons learned here would soon be applied to a far more complex terrain—the world of prescription medicines—where belief, once earned, would carry even greater weight.

Entering Glaxo

Taking Charge of the Family Products Division

When Tarun Gupta entered Glaxo, he was young by any corporate measure—and younger still by Glaxo's standards. Most contenders for senior marketing roles at the time carried decades of experience and the reassuring weight of hierarchy. Gupta carried something else: a reputation for judgment, a willingness to question orthodoxy, and an instinctive grasp of how brands earn trust. It was a gamble by Glaxo's leadership, and everyone in the room knew it.

The Family Products Division he was asked to lead was not in crisis, but it was drifting. Complan, Farex, Glaxose-D, and Ostermilk were established names, anchored in household familiarity rather than strategic clarity. Sales were steady, yet ambition was muted. The division operated more on habit than intent—competent, comfortable, and quietly vulnerable to more aggressive competitors.

Gupta understood immediately that this was not a portfolio problem. It was a mindset problem. The brands were being managed as commodities rather than convictions. Marketing existed to support sales, not to define direction. If Glaxo were to grow, the Family Products Division would need to become more than a caretaker of legacy—it would need to become a proving ground for modern marketing thinking.

From his first days, Gupta signaled a change in tempo. Meetings became sharper, shorter, and more demanding. He asked questions that unsettled assumptions: What does this brand stand for? Why should a mother choose us and not milk? What will the field say differently tomorrow? Comfort gave way to clarity.

Gupta also brought with him an unorthodox belief for the time—that mass media advertising and disciplined brand positioning were not the preserve of consumer goods companies alone. Nutrition, he believed, sat at the intersection of science and aspiration. It deserved the same strategic rigor as detergent or toothpaste, perhaps more.

Importantly, Gupta did not attempt to impose change through authority. He built credibility through preparation. His arguments were precise, his logic grounded in evidence, his expectations unmistakable. People began to sense that this was not enthusiasm; it was intent. The division was no longer reacting—it was being directed.

There was resistance, naturally. Youth invites skepticism. New ideas invite discomfort. Yet Gupta's approach was disarming in its seriousness. He did not overpromise or hedge. He spoke of investment horizons, not quick wins; of systems, not stunts. Gradually, the conversation shifted from whether change was needed to how fast it could be executed.

Taking charge of the Family Products Division marked Gupta's first opportunity to operate at scale within Glaxo. It allowed him to test ideas that had until then lived in fragments—about positioning, repetition, investment, and execution. More importantly, it placed him in an environment where success would be visible and failure unforgiving.

In retrospect, Glaxo's decision to back a young marketer proved decisive—not just for the company, but for the industry. By entrusting the Family Products Division to Tarun Gupta, Glaxo had unknowingly set in motion a transformation that would redefine how pharmaceutical marketing was practiced in India.

Nurturing Category Leaders

Making Complan and Farex Household Names

Turning a familiar product into a category leader requires more than visibility. It requires conviction—about what the brand stands for, whom it serves, and why it deserves loyalty over time. For Tarun Gupta, nurturing Complan and Farex into household names was not an exercise in amplification; it was an exercise in meaning-making.

Both brands entered the public consciousness before Gupta arrived, but their presence was diffuse. They were known, but not clearly understood. Complan was a "health drink," Farex a "baby food"—labels broad enough to include almost anything and precise enough to mean almost nothing. Gupta believed that leadership could not emerge from such vagueness. Categories are shaped not by volume alone, but by definition.

His first act of nurturing was to sharpen identity. Complan would no longer compete on taste or convenience. It would compete on nutritional adequacy. By framing the brand around the idea of completeness—twenty-three vital nutrients, compared with milk's nine—Gupta gave parents a concrete reason to choose Complan. The comparison was deliberate, almost confrontational, yet it remained respectful. It invited thought, not obedience.

Farex was treated with equal care. Gupta recognized that infant nutrition was a domain governed by anxiety and trust. Parents were not looking for novelty; they were looking for reassurance. Farex was positioned as a bridge between home feeding and structured nutrition—scientifically formulated, measured, and dependable. The brand spoke softly, but with authority.

What distinguished Gupta's approach was his refusal to chase ubiquity without coherence. Advertising was not scattershot. It was systematic. Messages were repeated until they settled. Visuals were consistent. Claims were restrained. The brands did not shout their superiority; they demonstrated it through clarity and persistence.

Gupta also understood that household names are built as much in distribution as in communication. Availability was treated as sacred. Retail presence was carefully and relentlessly expanded. Stock-outs were not seen as operational lapses but as brand failures. A product that could not be found, Gupta believed, could not be remembered.

Internally, he nurtured the brands by nurturing the people behind them. Sales teams were trained to articulate the brand story with confidence and consistency. Managers were held accountable not just for numbers, but for message integrity. The "wave-after-wave" discipline ensured that nurturing was continuous rather than episodic.

Over time, the results became self-reinforcing. Complan and Farex ceased to be just options; they became defaults. They entered everyday language, kitchens, and pediatric conversations. Competitors were forced to define themselves in relation to them. This is the quiet mark of category leadership: when a brand shapes the terms of choice.

For Gupta, this success reaffirmed a belief he would carry forward into prescription marketing: that trust is built through repetition, respect, and restraint. Household names are not created through spectacle. They are cultivated—patiently, deliberately, and with unwavering clarity of purpose.

In nurturing Complan and Farex, Tarun Gupta demonstrated that leadership is not seized in a moment. It is grown, sustained, and protected—one disciplined decision at a time.

Chapter 5

The 30-Day Blueprint – Mapping the Future

Strategy Is a Design Problem

When Tarun Gupta rewrote Glaxo's future in thirty days, he was not performing an act of rescue. He was solving a design problem.

The organization was not short of effort, intelligence, or goodwill. What it lacked was structure. Strategy existed as an aspiration. Execution existed as an activity. Results appeared sporadically, with no reliable link between intent and outcome.

Gupta's response was to separate what had been dangerously fused.

He insisted that strategy, implementation, and results be treated as three distinct responsibilities—each requiring different skills, rhythms, and measures. By explicitly assigning ownership, he removed ambiguity. Strategy could no longer hide behind execution. Execution could no longer blame the strategy. Results could no longer be explained away.

This separation was not bureaucratic. It was clarifying.

Once roles were clear, conversations changed. Meetings moved from justification to diagnosis. Accountability became structural rather than personal. Most importantly, learning became cumulative.

The insight behind the 30-day blueprint was deceptively simple:

Organizations do not fail because people are incapable—they fail because roles are poorly designed.

Strategy, Gupta believed, was not a visioning exercise.

It was an act of organizational architecture.

And architecture, once corrected, allowed performance to follow.

Crises rarely announce themselves with drama. More often, they arrive as a slow erosion of confidence—missed targets explained away, declining morale disguised as routine, strategy reduced to habit. When Tarun Gupta was asked to examine one such situation at Glaxo, he did not request months of data or a procession of committees. He asked for thirty days.

The assignment took him to Calcutta, then the nerve center of Glaxo's pharmaceutical operations. What he encountered there was not incompetence, but drift. Plans existed, but they were fragmented. Responsibility was shared so widely that it belonged to no one. Sales blamed marketing, marketing blamed the field, and the field quietly absorbed the consequences. The organization was busy, but it was not moving.

Gupta approached the problem with the instincts of a diagnostician rather than a rescuer. His first week was spent listening—intently, systematically—to everyone who touched the business. He spoke with field representatives, first-line managers, regional heads, and senior executives. He did not ask what they thought the problem was; he asked what they did every day. Patterns emerged quickly. Effort was abundant. Direction was not.

The second phase was analytical, but not abstract. Gupta mapped the business as it was actually being run, not as it was described in presentations. Where did decisions originate? Where did they stall? Which activities created momentum, and which merely consumed time? He discovered that strategy and execution existed in parallel universes, occasionally intersecting but rarely aligned.

By the third week, Gupta had begun to draft what would later be remembered as the "30-Day Blueprint." It was not a vision document. It was a working plan—concrete, sequenced, and unapologetically practical. Each objective was tied to a specific action. Each action had an owner. Each owner had a deadline. Ambiguity was removed not through rhetoric, but through design.

What made the blueprint radical was its insistence on simultaneity. Gupta rejected the idea that strategy must precede execution in a linear fashion. Planning, he argued, was meaningless unless it anticipated how work would actually be done. The blueprint, therefore, addressed three dimensions at once: what the company would aim to achieve, how it would mobilize people to achieve it, and how success would be measured along the way.

There was resistance. The clarity exposed weakness. Long-standing power centers found themselves bypassed. Comfort zones evaporated. Yet Gupta did not negotiate the architecture. He believed that organizations, like brands, require coherence before they can earn confidence.

By the end of thirty days, Glaxo did not have a perfect plan. It had something more valuable: a shared understanding of direction and discipline. People knew what mattered. They knew what was expected. And perhaps most importantly, they knew how their daily work contributed to the future.

The "30-Day Blueprint" became more than a turnaround exercise. It became a template for how Gupta thought about change itself. Transformation, he learned, did not require grand timelines or heroic interventions. It required attention, structure, and the courage to make a decision.

In mapping Glaxo's future in thirty days, Tarun Gupta demonstrated a principle that would guide the rest of his career: that clarity, delivered quickly and enforced consistently, is the most powerful tool a leader possesses.

A Week in Calcutta

Redrafting the Strategy for a Sinking Ship

Calcutta did not feel like a headquarters in distress. It felt worse than that. It felt resigned.

When Tarun Gupta arrived, there were no visible emergencies—no shouting, no panic, no dramatic collapses. The machinery was still running. Sales calls were being made. Reports were being filed. Yet beneath this surface activity lay a quiet acceptance that the pharmaceutical business was slipping, and that slipping had become normal.

Gupta sensed it within the first few days. Conversations were polite, careful, and circular. Problems were acknowledged, but never owned. Strategy existed in fragments—half-formed ideas scattered across departments that rarely converged. The organization was working hard, but not together. It was a sinking ship whose crew had learned to adjust to the tilt.

Rather than convene formal reviews, Gupta chose immersion. He spent his first days listening—on sales floors, in regional offices, and in unstructured conversations that revealed more than any presentation could. He asked disarmingly: "What do you do first when you arrive at work?" Who do you wait for before making a decision? What happens when something goes wrong? The answers exposed a system paralysed by diffusion of responsibility.

What emerged was not a lack of intelligence or effort, but a lack of alignment. Marketing is planned without ownership. Sales executed without conviction. Results were measured, but never interpreted. Everyone was busy managing tasks; no one was managing outcomes.

Midweek, Gupta began to sketch—not on charts or slides, but on paper. He mapped how decisions should flow, how priorities should cascade, and how accountability could be restored without humiliation. The exercise was not cosmetic. It cut through layers of legacy thinking that had accumulated over the years.

By the fourth day, the outline of a new strategy had taken shape. It was stark in its simplicity. Fewer priorities. Clear ownership. Unambiguous links between strategy and field action. Gupta resisted the temptation to be comprehensive. He believed that a plan that could not be remembered could not be executed.

The final days were spent testing the draft against reality. Gupta walked it through with managers and field leaders, not as a decree but as a challenge. Can you do this? What will stop you? What needs to change for this to work? Feedback was incorporated, not to dilute the plan, but to harden it.

By the end of the week, the ship had not yet turned—but it had a compass. People could see the direction. They could locate themselves within the plan. The sense of inevitability began to lift, replaced by something fragile but powerful: belief.

The week in Calcutta became legend not because it saved Glaxo overnight, but because it demonstrated what leadership looks like under pressure. Gupta did not bring theatrics or slogans. He brought attention, structure, and the willingness to decide.

In redrafting strategy for a sinking ship in a single week, Tarun Gupta reaffirmed a principle he would later teach relentlessly: that organizations do not fail from lack of ideas, but from lack of clarity—and that clarity, when delivered decisively, can still change the course.

The Three-Team Concept

Strategy, Implementation, and Results

One of Tarun Gupta's sharpest observations, forged during the Calcutta turnaround, was deceptively simple: most organizations fail not because they lack talent, but because they confuse roles. Strategy is discussed by everyone, execution is assumed by someone else, and results are reviewed after the fact—by people no longer connected to either. The Three-Team Concept was Gupta's answer to this quiet dysfunction.

At its core, the idea separated thinking from doing—not to create silos, but to enforce accountability. Gupta believed that clarity of responsibility was the first condition for performance. When everyone owns everything, nothing is owned at all.

The Strategy Team was responsible for intent. Its task was not to generate options endlessly, but to make choices. It defined what the organization would pursue and, just as importantly, what it would not. Gupta insisted that the strategy be articulated in language simple enough to be repeated without distortion. A strategy that could not survive retelling, he believed, was already compromised.

The Implementation Team owned the translation. This was where most strategies failed, and Gupta knew it. Implementation was not a mechanical exercise; it required judgment, adaptation, and discipline. The team's role was to convert intent into action—campaigns into calls, plans into behaviors. They were not allowed to reinterpret strategy, only to operationalize it. Ambiguity was escalated, not improvised.

The Results Team served as the organization's conscience. Its function was not to police, but to illuminate. Data was collected, interpreted, and fed back into the system quickly enough to matter. Gupta was emphatic that results must inform action, not merely record performance. Lagging indicators were supplemented with early signals—so correction could occur before damage became permanent.

What made the Three-Team Concept effective was not the separation itself, but the discipline of interaction. Each team had defined handoffs and explicit feedback loops. Strategy did not disappear once plans were written. Implementation was not shielded from scrutiny. Results were not weaponized for blame.

This structure also dismantled informal power centers. Authority was no longer derived from proximity to senior leadership, but from clarity of role. Decisions flowed through design, not personality. For organizations accustomed to ambiguity as a form of protection, this was unsettling—and transformative.

Gupta understood that people resist structure not because it limits freedom, but because it exposes responsibility. The Three-Team Concept did exactly that. It made accountability visible without making it punitive.

In time, the framework became a template—not just for Glaxo, but for Gupta's broader philosophy of management. He would later teach that successful organizations are not those with the smartest strategies, but those that know who is responsible for thinking, who is responsible for doing, and who is responsible for learning.

By separating strategy, implementation, and results—while binding them into a single system—Tarun Gupta gave organizations something rare: the ability to act with coherence, adapt with intelligence, and improve with intention.

Vignette: The Reputation of the Tie

Discipline Arrives at Burroughs Wellcome

In organizations, culture often announces itself long before strategy does. At Burroughs Wellcome, it arrived in the form of a tie.

When Tarun Gupta was appointed to take charge, there were no formal memos, no declarations of reform, no speeches about discipline. Yet within days, a subtle unease spread through corridors and field offices alike. People straightened their posture. Meetings began on time. Conversations became more deliberate. The reason was not policy—it was presence.

Gupta was known for a certain precision in appearance. The tie, always correctly chosen and immaculately worn, was not an affectation. It was a signal. To those who had worked with him before, it conveyed something unmistakable: expectations had changed.

In an industry where informality often blurred into indifference, Gupta treated professionalism as a form of respect—both for the work and for those who did it. He believed that discipline did not begin with targets or controls, but with self-regard. How one presented oneself, he felt, reflected how seriously one took responsibility.

The reputation traveled faster than the man himself. Field staff spoke of him before meeting him. Managers adjusted their behavior preemptively. The tie became shorthand for a broader ethos: preparation would be expected, excuses would not be indulged, and clarity would replace casualness.

What made the vignette enduring was its quietness. Gupta did not enforce discipline through reprimand. He embodied it. There was no scolding for missed standards—only a calm expectation that standards would be met. In such an environment, mediocrity felt exposed.

The effect at Burroughs Wellcome was immediate. Meetings sharpened. Reporting improved. Decisions accelerated. People began to take pride not just in outcomes, but in process. Discipline, once associated with fear, was reframed as professionalism.

Years later, colleagues would recall "the tie" with a mix of amusement and admiration. It had come to represent something larger than attire. It symbolized a leadership style that valued order without rigidity, authority without noise, and seriousness without severity.

In that sense, the reputation of the tie captured Tarun Gupta's genius in miniature. He understood that culture shifts not through slogans, but through signals—and that sometimes, the most powerful signal is the quietest one in the room.

Chapter 6

From Sales Promotion to Product Management

The Product Manager as "Mini-CEO"

Gupta's redefinition of the product manager role was radical for its time.

Product managers were no longer custodians of brochures. They were owners of strategy, stewards of investment, and integrators of sales, science, and communication.

This idea—now taken for granted—was revolutionary in an era when pharma marketing was largely tactical. Gupta did not invent the role; he gave it dignity and consequence.

When Tarun Gupta turned his attention to the machinery of pharmaceutical marketing, he identified a flaw so fundamental that it had gone largely unquestioned: marketing was being mistaken for promotion. In many organizations, including Glaxo at the time, the marketing function existed primarily to produce materials, support the sales force, and react to competitive moves. Strategy, when it appeared at all, was episodic and detached. Gupta believed this was not merely inefficient—it was dangerous.

Sales promotion, by its nature, is tactical. It responds to targets, quarters, and immediate pressures. Product management, as Gupta envisioned it, was something altogether different. It required ownership across time. It demanded responsibility not just for what was said today, but for what the brand would mean tomorrow. The shift from one to the other would alter the organization's center of gravity.

Gupta's first act was definitional. He articulated the role of the product manager as a "mini-CEO"—a phrase that unsettled more than it inspired at first. This was not a metaphor. He meant it literally. The product manager would be accountable for strategy, investment, positioning, execution, and results. Brochures were incidental. Judgment was central.

This redefinition exposed the inadequacy of existing structures. Product managers had been trained as coordinators, not leaders. They managed timelines, not outcomes. Gupta addressed this by changing expectations before changing people. Planning cycles became more rigorous. Assumptions were challenged publicly. Decisions were documented and revisited. The comfort of ambiguity evaporated.

Gupta also severed the reflexive dependency on sales. Marketing, he insisted, must lead rather than follow. Sales execution would always matter, but it could not substitute for strategic clarity. This rebalancing was delicate. Sales teams, long accustomed to dominance, resisted. Gupta did not confront them directly. Instead, he built systems that made leadership visible through results.

The transformation extended to how success was measured. Activity metrics gave way to brand health indicators. Market share, prescription behavior, and message recall began to matter more than volume alone. Product managers were taught to interpret data, not just present it. This analytical rigor elevated marketing from craft to discipline.

Perhaps most disruptive was Gupta's intolerance for cosmetic work. Visual aids that looked impressive but said little were discarded. Campaigns without clear intent were rejected. Product managers learned that clarity was not optional—it was the price of authority.

Over time, the shift took hold. Product management became aspirational rather than administrative. Talented individuals gravitated toward the role because it offered consequence, not comfort. The organization began to think in horizons rather than quarters.

In moving Glaxo from sales promotion to product management, Tarun Gupta was not introducing a new function. He was restoring an old idea: that brands require stewardship. The change laid the groundwork for everything that followed—from disciplined detailing to data-driven decision-making—and it cemented Gupta's reputation as a leader who did not merely improve systems, but redefined them.

Redefining the Role

The Product Manager as a "Mini-CEO"

When Tarun Gupta described the product manager as a "mini-CEO," the phrase landed with a jolt. In an industry accustomed to equating marketing with materials and coordination, the idea sounded almost extravagant. Yet Gupta meant it with precision, not flourish. He was naming a responsibility that already existed but had never been fully acknowledged.

In Gupta's view, a brand was a business in miniature. It had a purpose, a market, a set of customers, competitors, and a finite pool of resources. To manage it piecemeal—one brochure here, one promotion there—was to abdicate leadership. Someone had to own the whole, and that someone was the product manager.

This ownership began with a strategy. The mini-CEO was expected to define where the brand would play and how it would win. Not in slogans, but in choices. What indication would be prioritized? Which message would be repeated? Where would investment be concentrated—and where would it deliberately not be spent? Gupta had little tolerance for strategies that attempted to please everyone. Focus, he believed, was the first test of leadership.

Ownership extended to investment. Product managers were no longer shielded from financial reality. They were expected to understand margins, defend budgets, and justify long-term spending. Gupta insisted that they think like stewards, not spenders. Every rupee committed to a brand was a bet on its future, and the mini-CEO was accountable for that bet.

The role also demanded mastery of execution. Gupta rejected the notion that execution could be delegated without understanding. Product managers had to know how their plans translated in the field—how messages sounded in a doctor's clinic, how materials were used, how representatives struggled or succeeded. Authority, in Gupta's system, flowed from familiarity with reality, not from hierarchy.

Equally important was accountability for results. Success could not be attributed solely to sales performance, nor failure excused by market conditions.

The mini-CEO owned outcomes, good or bad. Data was not a shield; it was a mirror. Product managers learned to read it honestly and act decisively on it.

This redefinition altered behavior as much as structure. Product managers began preparing differently, speaking with greater confidence, and accepting discomfort as part of the role. Meetings shifted in tone. Questions became sharper. Decisions carried weight.

For many, the role became so demanding as to be intimidating. Gupta was unapologetic. He believed that dignity in work arises from consequence, not convenience. Those who thrived under the mini-CEO model emerged as leaders capable of thinking across silos, balancing ambition with discipline.

In redefining the product manager as a mini-CEO, Tarun Gupta was not inflating titles. He was restoring coherence to marketing leadership. The idea would ripple outward—shaping careers, influencing organizational design, and setting a standard that would endure long after individual campaigns faded.

It was, in essence, Gupta's answer to a simple question: If a brand is worth building, who is truly responsible for it?

The "Cabin Coup"

Clearing LBL Cobwebs and Empowering Talent

In many pharmaceutical organizations, power does not always reside in formal titles. It accumulates quietly—in cabins, in filing cabinets, in habits that go unchallenged because they are familiar. At Glaxo, Tarun Gupta discovered one such accumulation: LBLs—leave-behind literature that had ceased to inform but continued to dominate.

LBLs were everywhere. They filled cupboards, dictated conversations, and consumed disproportionate time and money. Yet few could explain what they actually achieved. They had become a proxy for productivity: something tangible to distribute, something visible to justify effort. Gupta saw them for what they were—a fog that obscured thinking and diluted accountability.

The "Cabin Coup" began not as a dramatic purge, but as a pointed question posed behind closed doors: Why are we doing this? When answers dissolved into habit and convenience, Gupta acted.

He ordered a systematic clearing of LBL stockpiles. Cabinets were opened. Shelves were emptied. Materials were scrutinized not for design, but for purpose. What could not be explained was discarded. The act was symbolic and unsettling. For some, it felt like an erasure of legacy. For others, it was liberation.

But Gupta's intent went beyond decluttering. By removing the crutch of LBLs, he forced a deeper reckoning. Representatives could no longer rely on brochures to speak for them. Product managers could no longer hide behind paper. The conversation shifted from what we give to what we say.

This shift created space for talent to surface.

Individuals like K. S. Ramanathan, long constrained by ornamental roles, suddenly found room to think and lead. Without the noise of excessive materials, clarity became currency. Ideas mattered again. Judgment was visible. Those who had substance rose quickly.

The coup also recalibrated power within the organization. Authority moved away from those who controlled materials and toward those who could articulate strategy. Cabins lost their mystique. Conversations grew sharper. Decisions accelerated.

Gupta understood that empowerment often requires subtraction. By removing clutter—physical and intellectual—he allowed capability to emerge. The "Cabin Coup" was not about centralizing control; it was about restoring purpose.

In retrospect, the episode captured Gupta's managerial philosophy in microcosm. He believed that systems ossify when comfort replaces curiosity, and that leadership sometimes demands unsettling the familiar to reveal the essential.

Clearing the LBL cobwebs was not an attack on creativity. It was a defense of thinking. And in empowering talent through subtraction, Tarun Gupta once again demonstrated that real change often begins not by adding more—but by having the courage to remove what no longer serves.

Chapter 7

Unity of Command – Eliminating Power Centers

Structure Resolves Conflict

When Tarun Gupta eliminated overlapping power centers, he was not asserting authority. He was removing ambiguity.

Organizations often attribute internal conflict to personalities, politics, or culture. Gupta saw it differently. In his experience, most conflict was structural, not personal. When roles overlap, accountability blurs. When reporting lines are unclear, influence replaces responsibility. When authority is shared without clarity, decision-making becomes negotiation.

By aligning sales firmly under marketing and eliminating redundant roles, Gupta restored unity of command. This did not weaken the organization; it strengthened it. Decisions became faster because ownership was clear. Disagreements became productive because they occurred within defined boundaries.

Importantly, Gupta understood that unity of command was not about centralization. It was about coherence. Strategy, execution, and feedback had to speak to each other without distortion.

The result was not silence, but focus.

The lesson was enduring:

When structure is clear, conflict diminishes; when structure is ambiguous, conflict multiplies.

Gupta believed that leadership was most visible not in arbitration, but in designing systems that made arbitration unnecessary.

As Tarun Gupta's reforms at Glaxo gathered momentum, a deeper structural problem came into view—one that no amount of marketing brilliance could compensate for. Authority was fragmented. Decisions emerged from multiple centers, often in conflict with one another. Sales answered to one hierarchy, marketing to another. Influence traveled sideways, diagonally, and sometimes not at all. The organization was functioning, but it was not aligned.

Gupta recognized the danger immediately. When power is dispersed without clarity, accountability dissolves. Strategies are diluted in translation. Execution becomes negotiable. People learn to navigate politics rather than pursue outcomes. For an organization attempting transformation, this was fatal.

The principle Gupta invoked was an old one, but rarely enforced: unity of command. It did not mean authoritarian control. It meant coherence. Every function would know where authority resided, how decisions flowed, and who was responsible when results fell short.

At the heart of the problem was the role of the All-India Sales Manager—a position that had evolved into a parallel power center. Nominally responsible for execution, the role often overruled marketing intent, reshaped field priorities, and diluted strategic focus. The result was predictable: confusion masked as flexibility.

Gupta's solution was decisive and controversial. He removed the redundancy. Sales would align directly under the marketing strategy, not alongside it. The move was less about hierarchy and more about accountability. If marketing defined direction, it would also own outcomes. Sales would execute with clarity, not contradiction.

Resistance was immediate. Power, once granted, is rarely surrendered gracefully. Critics warned of overcentralization. Others predicted demoralization. Gupta listened, but he did not relent. He understood that half-measures would only entrench the problem.

The impact was swift. Decision-making accelerated. Field priorities stabilized. Sales teams no longer received mixed signals. Marketing plans, once theoretical, began to translate consistently into action. Unity of command replaced negotiation with execution.

More subtly, the change altered behavior. Managers stopped building empires and started building capability. Conversations shifted from influence to impact. Success could be traced back to decisions, not personalities.

Gupta was careful to distinguish unity from uniformity. Local judgment was preserved, but within a clear strategic frame. The field was not silenced; it was synchronized.

By eliminating power centers, Tarun Gupta did more than reorganize reporting lines. He restored coherence to leadership. The chapter stands as a reminder that transformation is as much about removing structural obstacles as it is about introducing new ideas—and that clarity of command, when thoughtfully applied, can liberate an organization to perform at its best.

The Redundant All-India Sales Manager

In theory, the All-India Sales Manager was meant to be the fulcrum of execution—the single point through which national priorities translated into field action. In practice, the role had drifted into something far more ambiguous and far less useful. By the time Tarun Gupta examined the structure closely, the position no longer clarified authority; it complicated it.

The problem was not the individuals who held the role. Many were experienced, committed, and deeply knowledgeable about the field. The problem was structural. The All-India Sales Manager existed as a parallel command—neither fully accountable for strategy nor fully responsible for outcomes. Marketing sets direction. Sales owned numbers. And in between sat a role that mediated, modified, and often muted intent.

Gupta observed how this played out in everyday decisions. Marketing plans were reviewed, approved, and then reinterpreted before being sent to the field. Priorities shifted subtly but decisively. What was meant to be a focused campaign became a compromise. Accountability blurred. When results disappointed, explanations flowed easily, but ownership did not.

The redundancy lay not in the workload, but in the overlap. The All-India Sales Manager duplicated authority without adding clarity. Instead of accelerating execution, the role slowed it. Instead of strengthening discipline, it introduced discretion where none was needed.

Gupta believed that effective organizations require a clean line of sight—from intent to action to result. The existence of an intermediary power center disrupted that line. It allowed the strategy to be negotiated rather than executed. For a company striving to professionalize marketing, this was an unacceptable risk.

Eliminating the role was therefore not an act of consolidation, but of alignment. Sales execution would report directly to marketing leadership.

Direction would be singular. Feedback would be immediate. Success and failure would be traceable.

Predictably, the move unsettled the system. Roles that had once conferred influence now disappeared. Yet what replaced them was not vacuum, but clarity. Sales teams knew whose direction to follow. Marketing could no longer disown outcomes. Responsibility became visible.

Gupta's handling of the issue revealed his broader philosophy: organizations do not suffer from too little leadership, but from too many leaders operating without coherence. Removing the redundant All-India Sales Manager was not about reducing hierarchy; it was about restoring unity of purpose.

In stripping away this intermediary layer, Tarun Gupta reaffirmed a principle he would later teach repeatedly: that structure is strategy, and that clarity of command is not a constraint on performance—it is its foundation.

Ending Internal Bickering through Structural Clarity

Internal conflict, Tarun Gupta believed, rarely arises from personality alone. More often, it is manufactured by structure—by blurred roles, overlapping authority, and incentives that pull people in different directions. At Glaxo, years of incremental compromise had produced exactly such an environment. Disagreements were frequent, decisions slow, and outcomes diluted. Bickering had become a substitute for accountability.

Gupta did not attempt to resolve these tensions through persuasion or diplomacy. He addressed their source. The organization, he observed, had been designed to encourage negotiation over execution. Marketing and sales operated with intersecting mandates but without a shared hierarchy. Success was claimed collectively; failure was owned by no one.

The remedy was structural clarity.

By redefining reporting lines and enforcing unity of command, Gupta removed the ambiguity that allowed conflict to flourish. Roles were made explicit. Decision rights were clarified. The question Who decides?—so often avoided—was answered unambiguously. With clarity came consequence.

The immediate effect was unsettling. Conversations that once thrived on interpretation lost their footing. Informal power brokers found themselves exposed. Yet over time, the atmosphere shifted. Meetings became shorter. Arguments, when they occurred, focused on substance rather than turf. Energy once spent on internal alignment was redirected toward the market.

Gupta understood that bickering is often a rational response to uncertainty. When authority is unclear, individuals protect territory. By making authority visible, he reduced the need for defense. People could disagree within defined boundaries, without destabilizing the system.

Structural clarity also altered incentives. Success could no longer be claimed without ownership. Failure could no longer be deflected. Teams began to collaborate not because they were urged to, but because the structure required it.

In ending internal bickering through design rather than decree, Tarun Gupta demonstrated a rare managerial insight: that harmony is not achieved by asking people to behave better, but by building systems that make good behavior inevitable.

What emerged was not silence, but focus. Not conformity, but coherence. And in that clarity, Glaxo found the discipline it needed to move forward—unburdened by internal noise and aligned around purpose.

Part III

The Science of the "Clinic" – Professionalizing the Field

The Field Is Not a Stage

Tarun Gupta rejected the idea that the field force existed to perform. In his view, every interaction with a doctor was not a presentation, but a professional exchange—one that demanded preparation, restraint, and respect.

He believed the clinic was not a marketplace, but a place of judgment. The representative's role was not to impress, persuade, or entertain, but to assist decision-making. This distinction changed everything. Words mattered. Brevity mattered. Accuracy mattered. So did the discipline to stop speaking once the point was made.

Gupta often reminded his teams that doctors did not owe them attention. Attention had to be earned—through clarity of thinking and economy of expression. Excess, whether in language, visuals, or claims, was disrespectful.

By reframing the field as a professional space rather than a promotional arena, Gupta introduced science into a domain where theatrics had prevailed. Execution became quieter, more consistent, and more credible. Trust replaced novelty.

The principle was simple and unforgiving

When the field behaves like a profession, the brand is treated like one.

For Tarun Gupta, the clinic was never just a destination on a call plan. It was the crucible in which all marketing intent was tested—and often found wanting. Strategies could be elegant, messages compelling, and materials beautifully designed, but none of it mattered if the moment in the clinic collapsed into confusion, verbosity, or indifference. If pharmaceutical marketing was to mature as a discipline, Gupta believed, it had to begin where it ended: in the doctor's room.

This conviction marked a decisive shift in his thinking. Until then, much of marketing reform had focused on planning, positioning, and structure. Part III turns the lens toward execution—not as a tactical afterthought, but as a science in its own right. Gupta rejected the romantic notion that field performance was an art best left to individual flair. Variability, he argued, was not creativity; it was risk.

Professionalizing the field required standardization without dehumanization. Gupta set out to define what good looked like—clearly, repeatably, and at scale. He examined how stories were told, how visuals were used, how data-informed conversations were conducted, and how representatives prepared for each call. Every element was subject to scrutiny, not to constrain performance, but to elevate it.

The clinic, in Gupta's framework, was a system with its own constraints: limited time, competing demands, and cognitive overload. Respecting these constraints was not optional. It was the first rule of professionalism. Messages had to be concise. Visual aids had to guide rather than distract. Evidence had to be relevant, not exhaustive.

Part III traces how Gupta applied rigor to what had long been treated as instinct. He introduced minimum viable standards, disciplined narratives, and feedback loops that connected field behavior to outcomes. He replaced improvisation with preparation, clutter with clarity, and habit with intention.

What emerged was a redefinition of the medical representative—not as a courier of information, but as a professional communicator. Someone who understood not just the product, but the context in which it was discussed. Someone who could be trusted to represent the brand with consistency and judgment.

The clinic's science was not about control. It was about respect—for the doctor's time, for the brand's promise, and for the representative's craft. In professionalizing the field, Tarun Gupta closed the loop between strategy and reality, ensuring that what was imagined in planning rooms could survive—and succeed—where it mattered most.

This part of the book captures the moment when pharmaceutical marketing stopped hoping for excellence in execution—and began designing for it.

Chapter 8

The Art of the Story – Redefining the Visual Aid

The 40-Word Rule

If a message could not be delivered in forty words, Tarun Gupta believed it had not yet been understood.

The rule was not about brevity. It was about discipline.

By forcing marketers to compress their thoughts, Gupta ensured clarity for the field—and respect for the doctor's time. The rule became a quality filter, separating understanding from verbosity.

By the time Tarun Gupta turned his attention to visual aids, they had become the most overproduced and least examined artifacts of pharmaceutical marketing. Glossy, crowded, and dutifully distributed, they were treated as proof of effort rather than instruments of understanding. Gupta saw a deeper problem. The industry had mistaken visibility for communication.

Visual aids, in his view, were not meant to impress. They were meant to structure a conversation. Yet most had become repositories of everything a marketer wanted to say and nothing a doctor had time to absorb. Pages were dense with claims, charts, and qualifiers, forcing representatives to read rather than engage. The story, if it existed at all, was buried beneath ornamentation.

Gupta approached the issue as a storyteller rather than a designer. He believed that every effective detailing aid should answer three questions with ruthless clarity: What is the point? Why should I care? What should I remember? Anything that did not serve these questions was excess.

His first move was subtraction. Slides were stripped down. Visuals were simplified. Messages were reduced to their essence. This was not an aesthetic exercise. It was a cognitive one. Gupta understood that attention in a clinic is scarce and fragmented. A visual aid that demanded effort would be ignored.

He also challenged the assumption that more pages meant more persuasion. Gupta argued that a well-told story unfolds sequentially, not simultaneously. Each visual was designed to carry a single idea, delivered in a deliberate order. The representative's role was not to read, but to guide—using the aid as a scaffold, not a script.

This redefinition altered behavior in the field. Representatives had to understand the story deeply enough to narrate it naturally. Product managers had to think in narrative arcs rather than bullet points. The visual aid became a discipline in thinking, not just a deliverable.

Gupta was particularly intolerant of what he called visual clutter masquerading as science. Charts without context, data without implication, and claims without hierarchy were removed. Scientific credibility, he believed, came from clarity, not density. Respecting the doctor's intelligence meant respecting the doctor's time.

The transformation was met with skepticism at first. Simpler materials were mistaken for weaker ones. Gupta countered this by insisting on results. When doctors began to engage more actively, ask sharper questions, and recall messages more reliably, resistance faded.

In redefining the visual aid, Tarun Gupta elevated it from a prop to a narrative instrument. The art lay not in design, but in restraint. What remained after subtraction was a story that could travel intact—from product manager to representative to doctor.

This chapter captures one of Gupta's most enduring contributions: the recognition that, in pharmaceutical marketing, the most powerful stories are not the most elaborate ones but those that survive retelling.

Stopping LBL Waste

Why Brochures Belong in the Wastebasket

In the pharmaceutical industry, brochures had acquired an almost ceremonial status. They were designed, printed, shipped, displayed, and dutifully handed over—often without being read, remembered, or even opened. To many, they symbolized effort. To Tarun Gupta, they symbolized avoidance.

LBLs—leave-behind literature—had become a convenient substitute for thinking. When a message was unclear, another brochure was added. When a representative felt uncertain, a piece of paper was placed on the desk. Over time, clinics accumulated stacks of well-intentioned clutter, each piece competing for attention, ensuring none received it.

Gupta saw the waste immediately—not just financial, but cognitive as well. Brochures consumed budgets, but more importantly, they consumed focus. They encouraged representatives to rely on objects rather than understanding, and they allowed marketers to mistake production for progress. The question he asked was disarmingly simple: If this brochure disappeared, would the brand disappear with it?

His answer was often yes—and that troubled him deeply.

Gupta believed that communication in the clinic is an act of respect. Doctors do not need souvenirs; they need clarity. A brochure that cannot be summarized verbally is not an aid—it is an admission of confusion. By leaving behind paper, marketers were often leaving behind responsibility.

The decision to stop LBL waste was therefore philosophical as much as operational. Gupta challenged teams to justify every piece of literature not by aesthetics or compliance, but by purpose. If it did not advance the story, it was removed. If it duplicated what could be said more clearly, it was discarded.

The wastebasket became a symbol—not of austerity, but of discipline. Throwing away brochures was a declaration that understanding mattered more than artifacts. Representatives were forced to internalize the story. Product managers were forced to sharpen it. The brand's voice became human again.

There was discomfort. Habits were exposed. Some worried that without brochures, credibility would suffer. Gupta countered that credibility comes from coherence, not collateral. When representatives spoke confidently and consistently, doctors listened. When they relied on paper, doctors disengaged.

Over time, the absence of LBLs became a competitive advantage. Clinics felt less cluttered. Conversations felt more focused. Messages traveled farther because they were carried in memory rather than left on desks.

In consigning brochures to the wastebasket, Tarun Gupta was not rejecting tools. He was rejecting crutches. The move underscored a belief that ran through all his work: that marketing excellence begins not with what you leave behind, but with what the listener takes away.

The 40-Word Rule and Canned Detailing

Minimum Viable Quality

Tarun Gupta was deeply suspicious of verbosity. In his experience, long explanations rarely signaled depth; more often, they revealed uncertainty. Nowhere was this more evident than in detailing, where representatives—armed with information but lacking structure—attempted to say everything and ended up saying nothing.

The 40-word rule emerged as Gupta's corrective. If a brand's core message could not be delivered in forty words, he believed it had not yet been understood. The rule was not arbitrary. Forty words were enough to express an idea, but too few to hide confusion. It forced marketers to choose what mattered and discard what did not.

This discipline gave rise to what Gupta called canned detailing—a term often misunderstood. It did not imply robotic delivery or the suppression of personality. It implied standardization of quality. Just as manufacturing enforces tolerances to ensure consistency, canned detailing established a minimum viable standard for communication.

Gupta's concern was not brilliance at the top, but variability at scale. In the field, brilliance is uneven. Some representatives excel; many are average. Without structure, the average defines the brand experience. The 40-word rule ensured that even the weakest delivery met an acceptable threshold of clarity and correctness.

Canned detailing also protected the brand from distortion. Messages no longer drifted with mood or memory. The sequence stabilized. The logic held. Doctors heard the same story regardless of who visited or when. Over time, this consistency built familiarity—and familiarity built trust.

There was resistance, especially from those who equated freedom with effectiveness. Gupta challenged that assumption directly. Freedom without mastery, he argued, is noise. Structure, when internalized, liberates confidence. Once the 40-word spine was embedded, representatives could adapt tone and emphasis without compromising meaning.

The concept of minimum viable quality was central to Gupta's thinking. He accepted that not everyone could be exceptional, but he refused to accept inconsistency. The floor had to be raised before the ceiling could matter. Canned detailing did exactly that.

In practice, the rule transformed training, evaluation, and field performance. Representatives prepared differently. Managers coached more precisely. Conversations in clinics became shorter, sharper, and more respectful.

The 40-word rule endures not because it is clever, but because it is humane. It respects attention, enforces clarity, and acknowledges the realities of scale. In defining minimum viable quality for detailing, Tarun Gupta once again demonstrated his genius for translating abstract ideals into executable discipline—where it mattered most: in the moment of conversation.

Chapter 9

The Creative Workshop – Co-Creation with the Field

Creativity Improves When Authority Listens

Tarun Gupta did not believe that creativity resided in any one function. He believed it emerged when insight, experience, and craft met without hierarchy.

At a time when advertising ideas flowed in one direction—from agency to head office to the field—Gupta reversed the current. He invited field representatives, marketers, and creative professionals into the same room and treated their inputs as equally legitimate. The objective was not consensus, but relevance.

Field teams brought lived reality—what doctors asked, what they ignored, what they trusted. Head office contributed structure and continuity. Creative partners added imagination and expression. When these perspectives were fused early, campaigns gained coherence. When they were separated, creativity became decorative.

Gupta understood that creativity suffered most when it was insulated from consequences. By exposing ideas to those who would have to execute them, he imposed a quiet discipline. Weak ideas failed early. Strong ones survived.

The principle he demonstrated was enduring

Creativity improves when authority listens, and execution improves when creativity understands reality.

In this model, leadership did not direct creativity.

It designed the conditions in which creativity could be useful.

By the time Tarun Gupta turned to the question of creativity, he had already dismantled many of its comfortable myths. Creativity, he believed, did not reside exclusively in advertising agencies or head-office cabins. Nor was it a moment of inspiration detached from execution. In pharmaceutical marketing, creativity had to survive the field—or it was merely decoration.

The prevailing model placed creativity upstream and execution downstream. Campaigns were conceived in isolation, polished by specialists, and then handed to the field for implementation. When they failed, the field was blamed for poor execution, and when they succeeded, credit flowed upward. Gupta recognized the asymmetry immediately. He set out to reverse it.

The Creative Workshop was his Answer

Rather than treating the field as a delivery mechanism, Gupta invited it into the act of creation. Sales representatives, first-line managers, product managers, and advertising professionals were brought together—not to be briefed, but to collaborate. The workshop was not a presentation forum. It was a deliberately uncomfortable working session where ideas were tested against lived reality.

What distinguished these workshops was their rigor. Field participants were not asked what they liked. They were asked what worked. Which words held attention? Which visuals invited questions? Where did conversations falter? Gupta insisted that insight be earned through experience, not asserted through opinion.

Advertising agencies, accustomed to hierarchy, were initially unsettled. They found themselves challenged not by executives, but by representatives who knew the clinic intimately. Gupta welcomed the tension. He believed that creativity sharpened under constraint, and that friction between idea and execution was not a flaw—it was the point.

The outcome was a new kind of campaign. Messages became simpler because they had been tested verbally before being designed visually. Visual aids became more intuitive because they reflected how representatives actually spoke. Campaigns extended over time because the field had helped build them and, therefore, believed in them.

Co-creation also altered ownership. The field no longer felt like a recipient of strategy; it became a custodian of it. Compliance improved not because of enforcement, but because of authorship. People protect what they help create.

Gupta understood that creativity divorced from execution is fragile. By anchoring creativity in the field, he gave it resilience. Ideas could evolve without losing coherence. Adjustments could be made without losing intent.

The Creative Workshop marked a turning point in how pharmaceutical marketing was practiced. It blurred the line between thinking and doing—not by diluting either, but by aligning them. In doing so, Tarun Gupta demonstrated a principle that would echo throughout his career: that the most powerful ideas are not imposed from above, but built together—where reality is lived.

Vignette: The Advertising Summit

Fusing Field, Head Office, and Creative Minds

The Advertising Summit did not resemble a typical marketing meeting. There were no polished decks unveiled for approval, no agencies performing for applause, no senior executives pronouncing verdicts from the head of the table. Instead, it felt more like a workshop with the stakes of a boardroom—and that was precisely Tarun Gupta's intention.

For Gupta, the problem with most advertising was not creativity, but distance. Ideas were conceived far from the clinic, refined far from the field, and judged far from the consequences. The summit was designed to close that distance.

Sales executives sat alongside product managers, agency creatives, and senior leadership. Titles mattered less than experience. Conversations were direct, sometimes uncomfortable. Field executives spoke about what doctors actually said, not what briefs assumed they would say. Creatives defended ideas, but were also forced to listen—to cadence, to language, to resistance.

Gupta presided quietly. He did not arbitrate taste. He moderated relevance. When an idea sounded clever but unrepeatable, it was challenged. When a visual looked elegant but confused the field, it was reworked. The summit was not about winning arguments; it was about surviving reality.

What emerged from these sessions was not a single campaign, but a shared understanding. Campaigns became year-long programs rather than episodic bursts. Messages were fewer, clearer, and more durable. Creative ambition was not suppressed; it was focused.

The presence of the field irrevocably altered the tone. Sales executives were no longer passive recipients of advertising decisions. They became co-authors. This changed everything. Execution improved because belief improved. Creativity traveled intact because it had been forged in dialogue, not isolation.

Agencies, initially wary, began to appreciate the discipline. Constraints clarified direction. Feedback sharpened ideas. The work improved not despite the friction, but because of it.

The Advertising Summit became legendary not for its theatrics but for its outcomes. It institutionalized co-creation. It demonstrated that when field insight, strategic intent, and creative craft converge in the same room, marketing ceases to be aspirational and becomes executable.

In fusing field, head office, and creative minds, Tarun Gupta did more than improve campaigns. He redefined collaboration—and, in doing so, reminded the industry that the most enduring ideas are those that can be spoken, shown, and believed by the same people who must carry them forward.

The Exhibition of Ideas

Applying Marketing Principles to Visual Aids

Tarun Gupta believed that if marketing was truly a discipline, it had to be applied to its own tools. Visual aids, he observed, were rarely subjected to the rigor demanded of brands. They were designed, approved, and distributed—but seldom evaluated as marketing objects in their own right. The Exhibition of Ideas was his way of correcting that oversight.

Rather than reviewing visual aids in closed meetings, Gupta brought them into the open. Panels were displayed, sequences laid out, and campaigns presented as if they were competing brands in a marketplace. The exercise was not aesthetic. It was diagnostic. Each visual was examined through the same questions Gupta asked of any brand: What is the promise? What is the point of difference? What will be remembered?

This public scrutiny transformed the role of the visual aid. No longer could it hide behind compliance or creative intent. It had to earn attention. Visuals were judged not by how much information they carried, but by how clearly they communicated a single idea. Clutter was exposed. Redundancy became obvious. Confusion was no longer defensible.

Gupta insisted that sequencing mattered as much as content. A visual aid, he argued, should unfold like a story, not present like a catalogue. Each panel had to justify its place in the narrative. If removing a panel improved clarity, it was removed. If a visual required explanation, it failed the test.

The exhibition format also democratized critique. Field staff, product managers, and creatives evaluated the work together. Authority came from insight, not position. A representative who understood clinic dynamics could challenge a creative director—and often did. The result was not dilution, but refinement.

Over time, the Exhibition of Ideas became a proving ground. Only those visual aids that could withstand public examination reached the field. The process raised standards quietly but decisively. Visuals became simpler, stories tighter, and execution more confident.

By applying marketing principles to visual aids themselves, Tarun Gupta closed a loop the industry had long ignored. He reminded his teams that every artifact speaks—and that if a visual cannot communicate its value clearly, it has no place in a disciplined system.

The exhibition was not about display. It was about accountability. And in treating visual aids as brands that had to earn their keep, Gupta once again demonstrated his gift for turning philosophy into practice—one panel at a time.

Chapter 10

Prescription Auditing – The C-MARC Revolution

From Intuition to Evidence

Long before "data-driven marketing" became fashionable, Gupta sought proof.

By introducing prescription audits and panel data, he shifted discussions from anecdote to evidence. Brands could now be diagnosed, not guessed.

This marked a philosophical turning point: marketing was no longer art versus science—it was art informed by science

For much of its early history, pharmaceutical marketing operated on intuition. Brands were discussed in anecdotes, performance inferred from fragments, and competitive moves interpreted through rumor. Success was explained after the fact; failure was rationalized away. Tarun Gupta found this deeply unsatisfying. If marketing was to claim the status of a discipline, he believed, it had to submit itself to evidence.

The Introduction of Prescription Auditing Marked that Turning Point

Gupta's interest in data was not academic. He was not searching for precision for its own sake. He wanted visibility—a way to see what was actually happening between brands and doctors, beyond the comforting abstractions of sales numbers. Sales told him what had moved. Prescriptions, he believed, would tell him why.

The partnership with Professor Chitta Mitra and the creation of C-MARC—a prescription audit panel—was revolutionary for its time. Drawing inspiration from consumer panels used in industries like tobacco and FMCG, Gupta adapted the idea to the far more complex and sensitive terrain of medical practice. It was an audacious move. Many doubted whether doctors would participate or whether the data would be reliable. Gupta persisted.

What C-MARC delivered was not just numbers, but insight. For the first time, brands could see patterns of loyalty and switching. They could distinguish between growth driven by new prescriptions and growth cannibalized from competitors. They could observe how promotional intensity translated—or failed to translate—into prescribing behavior.

Most importantly, the data disrupted comforting narratives. Brands that appeared strong in sales revealed hidden fragility. Others, dismissed as weak, showed pockets of deep loyalty. Decisions that had once been defended by seniority now had to answer to evidence.

Gupta insisted that the data be used not as a weapon, but as a guide. C-MARC was designed to shorten learning cycles, not assign blame. Results were discussed openly, interpreted collectively, and acted upon quickly. Strategy became iterative. Campaigns could be adjusted mid-course. Assumptions could be tested rather than defended.

The cultural impact was profound. Marketing conversations changed tone. Opinions softened into hypotheses. Field feedback gained context. Managers learned to ask better questions, because they now had better answers.

The C-MARC revolution also reinforced Gupta's belief in humility as a managerial virtue. Data, he often reminded his teams, does not make decisions—it reveals reality. What leaders do with that reality defines their competence.

By institutionalizing prescription auditing, Tarun Gupta brought pharmaceutical marketing out of the realm of belief and into that of knowledge. It was not the end of judgment, but its refinement. And in doing so, he gave the industry a tool that would permanently alter how brands were understood, managed, and grown.

Pioneering Panel Data with Professor Chitta Mitra

When Tarun Gupta began exploring the use of panel data in pharmaceutical marketing, he was venturing into largely uncharted territory. At the time, the very idea that doctors 'prescribing behavior could be systematically observed, aggregated, and analyzed over time was viewed with skepticism—if not outright disbelief. Marketing, many felt, was too complex, too human, too situational to be captured in structured data. Gupta disagreed.

What he needed was not just a method, but a mind that could bridge rigor and relevance. He found that in Professor Chitta Mitra.

Mitra brought academic discipline without academic detachment. He understood statistics, sampling, and longitudinal analysis, but he was equally alert to context. Gupta respected this balance. Together, they shared a conviction that evidence should illuminate practice, not replace it. The challenge was not to reduce marketing to numbers, but to let numbers reveal patterns that intuition alone could not see.

The idea of a panel—the same set of doctors tracked consistently over time—was central. Gupta believed that one-off snapshots distorted reality. Brands were not won or lost in isolated moments, but through gradual shifts in habit. Only a panel could capture this movement: loyalty forming, erosion beginning, competitors encroaching quietly before anyone noticed.

Building such a system required trust. Doctors had to be willing participants. Data collection had to be discreet, ethical, and reliable. Mitra's academic credibility helped establish legitimacy, while Gupta's industry standing ensured relevance. Together, they designed a process that balanced methodological rigor with practical feasibility.

When the first sets of data emerged, their impact was immediate—and unsettling. Assumptions hardened over the years began to soften. Some brands discovered that growth was coming at the expense of internal cannibalization rather than competitive gain. Others learned that high promotional pressure was producing diminishing returns. Patterns of switching, once guessed at, could now be observed.

Gupta insisted that these insights not remain confined to analysts. They were brought into marketing discussions, field reviews, and strategy sessions. Data became a common language—not to end debate, but to elevate it. Arguments were no longer settled by seniority alone. Evidence had a seat at the table.

Professor Mitra's contribution ensured that the system retained credibility. The data could be questioned, but not dismissed. It had been thoughtfully designed, cautiously interpreted, and intelligently applied. For Gupta, this partnership validated a belief he had long held: that the most powerful innovations occur when academic rigor meets practical urgency.

Pioneering panel data was not an exercise in modernity. It was an act of discipline. By working with Professor Chitta Mitra to institutionalize longitudinal insight, Tarun Gupta helped move pharmaceutical marketing from anecdote to understanding—without losing sight of the human judgment at its core.

It was another quiet revolution: one that replaced certainty with curiosity, and instinct with informed choice.

Unpeeling the Onion

Understanding Switching and Doctor Behavior

When prescription audit data first began to flow in, many managers treated it as confirmation—evidence that validated what they already believed. Tarun Gupta saw something else entirely. To him, the data was not an answer; it was an invitation. An invitation to look beneath surface performance and ask why doctors chose one brand over another—and why they changed their minds.

He often described this process as unpeeling the onion. Each layer revealed a different truth, and none of them stood alone.

At the outermost layer were the visible numbers—market share, prescription volume, growth rates. These were comforting in their familiarity, but deceptive in their simplicity. A rising share could mask fragile loyalty. A declining brand might still command deep trust among a small but influential group of physicians. Gupta warned against treating these numbers as conclusions. They were merely symptoms.

The next layer exposed switching behavior. Panel data revealed that prescriptions did not move as monolithic blocks. They shifted gradually, often invisibly, from one brand to another. Gupta became fascinated by this movement. Was growth coming from new patients or from doctors abandoning a competitor? Was a decline the result of price, perception, availability, or silence?

As the layers peeled back further, patterns of habit emerged. Gupta recognized that doctors, like all professionals under pressure, rely on routines. Switching was rarely impulsive. It followed disruption—new evidence, persistent messaging, peer influence, or a breakdown in trust. Understanding these triggers required patience and humility. The data could show that switching occurred; interpretation was needed to understand why.

Gupta insisted that teams resist the urge to oversimplify. A doctor who switched was not disloyal; he was responding to a context. Effective marketing, Gupta believed, did not coerce change—it earned it, layer by layer.

Perhaps the most uncomfortable layer revealed self-inflicted wounds. Brands often lost share not because competitors were superior, but because messaging had become inconsistent, frequency had dropped, or field discipline had weakened. Data exposed these failures without drama, but with clarity.

Unpeeling the onion transformed how marketing conversations unfolded. Questions replaced assertions. Curiosity replaced defensiveness. Managers began to see doctor behavior not as resistance to be overcome, but as logic to be understood.

For Gupta, this was the true value of prescription auditing. It did not eliminate judgment; it refined it. By patiently peeling back layers of behavior, he taught marketers to respect complexity without being paralyzed by it.

In understanding switching and doctor behavior, Tarun Gupta once again demonstrated his core belief: that effective marketing begins not with persuasion, but with empathy—and that insight, like truth, reveals itself only to those willing to look beyond the surface.

Part IV

Cultivating Management Excellence

When a Man Becomes a Movement

Long after Tarun Gupta stepped away from corporate roles, his influence continued—through students, protégés, and systems that outlived him.

Tributes following his passing spoke less about the positions he held and more about the minds he shaped. In that distinction lies the measure of his legacy.

Tarun Gupta never believed that organizations are transformed by ideas alone. Ideas, he observed, travel only as far as the people entrusted to carry them. Systems can be designed, strategies articulated, and structures realigned—but without capable managers, none of it endures. Part IV turns to the question Gupta considered most consequential: how to build managers worthy of responsibility.

For Gupta, management excellence was not a matter of pedigree or polish. It was a discipline shaped by selection, training, and expectation. Too often, he felt, organizations promoted competence into comfort and mistook seniority for judgment. The result was predictable: capable individuals constrained by inadequate preparation, and systems weakened by uneven leadership.

Cultivating excellence began with choice. Gupta was exacting about who entered managerial roles. He looked beyond credentials to character, beyond fluency to resilience. The field, he believed, revealed truths that interviews could not. Those who thrived under pressure, listened well, and learned quickly were the ones worth investing in.

Once selected, managers were not indulged—they were developed. Gupta rejected episodic training in favor of continuous immersion. Learning, in his view, was not an event but a habit. Exposure to global thinking, rigorous debate, and real-world problems was essential. Managers were expected to read, question, and reflect—long after formal programs ended.

Equally important was how excellence was recognized. Gupta understood the symbolic power of reward. By celebrating achievement publicly and setting high thresholds for recognition, he sent a clear signal: standards mattered. Incentives were not consolation prizes; they were markers of distinction.

Part IV also examines Gupta's insistence on intellectual ambition. He wanted managers who could think beyond their immediate roles, who were comfortable with complexity, and who saw themselves as stewards of the organization's future. To cultivate such leaders, he brought the world into the company through speakers, journals, and relentless exposure to new ideas.

This section of the book explores the architecture Gupta built to sustain excellence: rigorous selection systems, demanding training philosophies, and cultural signals that reinforced dignity in work. It reveals a leader who understood that management is not inherited—it is constructed.

In cultivating management excellence, Tarun Gupta was doing more than building careers. He was building continuity. The systems he designed outlived his tenure because they were anchored in people who had learned not just what to do, but how to think.

Chapter 11

The Five-Stage Selection Process

Hiring for the Field, Not the Desk

Gupta famously said he looked for the "bloke," not the "gentleman."

The phrase was not anti-intellectual. It was anti-pretension. He believed the field demanded resilience, judgment, and humility—qualities rarely visible in polished interviews.

His five-stage selection process was designed to surface character, not credentials.

Tarun Gupta approached selection with the same seriousness he applied to strategy. In his view, few managerial decisions carried greater consequences than choosing who would lead in the field. Yet in most organizations, selection was treated as an administrative ritual—driven by résumés, first impressions, and polite interviews that revealed little about how a person would behave under pressure. Gupta believed this was an abdication of responsibility.

The Five-Stage Selection Process was his response. It was not designed to be efficient. It was designed to be revealing.

Gupta began with a simple premise: competence in the field cannot be inferred from polish in a room. Sales and marketing demand resilience, judgment, and the ability to learn quickly from imperfect situations. The process, therefore, unfolded over time, allowing candidates to be observed rather than assessed in a single moment.

The early stages focused on exposure. Candidates were placed in real environments—interacting with doctors, navigating territory constraints, responding to unpredictability. Gupta wanted to see how they listened, how they adapted, and how they handled discomfort. Knowledge gaps could be filled. Attitude could not.

Subsequent stages introduced evaluation under scrutiny. Candidates were asked to articulate what they had seen, not in abstract terms, but in actionable insight. Could they distinguish signal from noise? Could they explain behavior without blaming circumstance? Clarity of thought, Gupta believed, was the first marker of leadership potential.

The later stages tested judgment and integrity. Scenarios were designed to surface decision-making under ambiguity—ethical dilemmas, trade-offs between short-term gain and long-term trust. Gupta was explicit: character was not negotiable. Talent without integrity, he felt, was a liability.

Throughout the process, Gupta resisted premature closure. No single stage was decisive. Patterns mattered more than moments. Candidates who appeared impressive initially but deteriorated under sustained observation were screened out. Those who grew—who learned, reflected, and improved—rose steadily.

The Five-Stage Selection Process sent a powerful cultural signal. Entry into leadership was earned, not granted. The organization was willing to invest time and attention to get it right. Those selected emerged not only validated, but also aware of the standards they were expected to uphold.

In institutionalizing this process, Tarun Gupta professionalized not just hiring, but aspiration. He taught the organization that excellence begins long before performance reviews—with the courage to choose carefully, and the patience to observe deeply.

Finding the "Bloke," Not the "Gentleman"

When Tarun Gupta spoke of looking for the "bloke," not the "gentleman," he was not making a cultural provocation. He was making a managerial distinction. In an era when polish was often mistaken for potential, Gupta deliberately inverted the hierarchy of traits he valued.

The "gentleman," as Gupta called him, was articulate, agreeable, and impressive in controlled settings. He spoke fluently, knew the right answers, and navigated interviews with ease. Yet too often, Gupta found, this composure dissolved in the field—where ambiguity, rejection, and relentless repetition demanded something else entirely.

The "bloke," by contrast, was less refined and more resilient. He might lack sophistication, but he possessed sturdiness. He listened more than he spoke. He learned by doing. In the face of resistance, he adapted rather than retreated. For Gupta, these qualities mattered far more than presentation.

Pharmaceutical marketing, Gupta believed, was a craft practiced under pressure. The field exposed pretense quickly. Doctors did not reward elegance; they rewarded clarity and credibility. The "bloke" thrived here—not because he was clever, but because he was authentic and persistent.

This preference also reflected Gupta's democratic view of leadership. He believed talent was widely distributed, but opportunity was not. By looking past surface polish, he widened the pool of potential leaders. Many who might have been overlooked by conventional processes found space to grow.

The distinction carried an ethical dimension as well. Gupta was wary of individuals who performed well upward but disengaged downward. Leadership, in his view, required comfort across levels—respect for the field as much as for the boardroom.

Finding the "bloke" did not mean rejecting refinement. It meant postponing it. Skills could be taught. Confidence could be built. Character, Gupta believed, revealed itself early and endured.

In elevating the "bloke" over the "gentleman," Tarun Gupta made a quiet statement about merit. He chose substance over style, endurance over ease, and learning over display. It was a philosophy that shaped not just his teams, but the character of leadership across an industry.

Building Tomorrow's Area Sales Executives

Tarun Gupta did not view Area Sales Executives as intermediaries in a reporting chain. He saw them as the organization's fulcrum—the point at which strategy either translated into disciplined action or dissolved into improvisation. Building tomorrow's ASEs, therefore, was not a matter of promotion. It was an act of deliberate construction.

Gupta began by redefining the role's demands. An effective Area Sales Executive, in his view, was neither a super-salesperson nor a passive administrator. He was a manager of people, priorities, and performance—capable of holding the field to standards while absorbing complexity from above. This required judgment, not just energy.

Selection was only the first filter. Development was where Gupta invested most heavily. Newly appointed ASEs were immersed in structured learning on brand strategy, clinic behavior, data interpretation, and coaching skills. Gupta insisted that they understand why before enforcing what. Authority without understanding, he believed, bred compliance at best and cynicism at worst.

Field exposure remained central. Gupta discouraged desk-bound management. ASEs were expected to observe calls, listen to conversations, and diagnose problems in real time. Feedback was specific, immediate, and often uncomfortable. Vague encouragement had no place in Gupta's system.

He also trained ASEs to think laterally. Performance was not just about targets achieved, but about patterns emerging. Why was one territory improving while another stagnated? Why did one representative thrive under structure while another resisted it? These questions mattered more than raw numbers.

Crucially, Gupta taught ASEs to model the behavior they demanded. Discipline, preparation, and integrity were not optional. They were visible. An ASE who cut corners forfeited moral authority. One who upheld standards quietly earned them.

Over time, the results were evident. ASEs developed a shared language of performance. Coaching improved. Variability reduced. The field became more predictable—not in effort, but in quality.

Building tomorrow's Area Sales Executives was Gupta's way of future-proofing the organization. He understood that systems endure only when managers internalize them. By constructing leaders who could think, coach, and decide, he ensured that discipline would survive beyond his direct presence.

In doing so, Tarun Gupta demonstrated that leadership development is not about acceleration—it is about foundation. And the strongest foundations, he believed, are built patiently, one manager at a time.

Chapter 12

The Star Award Function – Treating Representatives Like Royalty

Recognition Signals What an Organization Values

Tarun Gupta did not view recognition as motivation. He viewed it as communication.

In his thinking, award functions were not morale-boosting exercises or celebratory rituals. They were moments of public signaling—clear statements about what the organization respected, rewarded, and expected. When done casually, recognition dilutes standards. When done deliberately, it reinforced them.

By treating high-performing representatives with dignity and ceremony—rather than excess or spectacle—Gupta elevated the role itself. Recognition was not about creating stars; it was about making excellence visible. The presence of senior leadership, the seriousness of the occasion, and the clarity of the criteria all mattered more than the prize.

Gupta was equally deliberate about thresholds. Incentives began only beyond full achievement. Meeting expectations was not exceptional—it was professional. Distinction began where commitment exceeded obligation.

The Underlying belief was Simple and Demanding

People rise to the standards that organizations choose to honor publicly.

For Gupta, recognition was never an emotional tool.

It was an architectural one—designed to align aspiration with discipline.

Tarun Gupta understood something that many leaders overlooked: recognition is not a reward—it is a signal. It tells an organization what it truly values. In an industry where field representatives often worked in isolation, were measured primarily by numbers, and were remembered only when targets were missed, Gupta saw an opportunity to redefine dignity in performance.

The Star Award Function was his response.

It was not conceived as a routine incentive ceremony. It was designed as a statement. By publicly and ceremonially elevating top-performing representatives, Gupta sought to do more than hand out trophies. He wanted to alter the psychological contract between the organization and the field.

The setting mattered. The structure mattered. The presence of senior leadership mattered. When representatives were flown in, accommodated with care, and recognized in front of the company's highest authority—including the global chairman—the message was unmistakable: excellence in the field was not peripheral; it was central.

Gupta was deliberate about who qualified. Awards did not begin at 90% or even 100% achievement. The threshold was 101 percent. This was not a numerical quirk. It was a philosophical line. Meeting expectations was the job. Exceeding them was a distinction.

The ceremony itself was marked by restraint. There was no theatrical excess, no inflated rhetoric. Names were called. Achievements were stated clearly. Applause was earned. The tone was respectful, not indulgent. Representatives felt seen—not flattered, but acknowledged.

What made the Star Award Function transformative was its ripple effect. Those recognized returned to the field with confidence and pride. Those who were not recognized understood the standards they were being measured against. The awards created aspiration without resentment.

Gupta also understood that symbolic recognition reinforces behavioral norms. By celebrating consistency, preparation, and professionalism, he shifted attention away from short-term heroics and toward sustained excellence. The field responded accordingly.

Treating representatives like royalty was not about extravagance. It was about respect. Gupta believed that people rise to the expectations placed upon them when those expectations are clear and credible.

In institutionalizing the Star Award Function, Tarun Gupta demonstrated that culture is shaped as much by what is celebrated as by what is controlled. By publicly and unapologetically honoring the field, he elevated not just individuals but the very idea of field excellence—and, in doing so, strengthened the foundation of the organization itself.

The Srinagar Milestone

The Srinagar Star Award function was remembered long after the applause faded—not because of where it was held, but because of what it redefined. In choosing Srinagar as the venue, Tarun Gupta was making a statement that went beyond logistics. He was signaling that excellence in the field deserved not just acknowledgment, but honor.

For many representatives, it was the first time their work had carried them so far from routine—out of territories and targets, into a setting that felt deliberately chosen and thoughtfully prepared. Srinagar was not a reward destination in the conventional sense. It was dignified, distinctive, and slightly unexpected. That, Gupta believed, was precisely the point.

The ceremony itself unfolded with restraint. There was no spectacle masquerading as motivation. Instead, there was formality, order, and presence. When the global chairman of Glaxo stood before the assembled representatives, the organization's hierarchy briefly inverted. Those who usually reported upward were now being addressed directly, their achievements acknowledged at the highest level.

Gupta understood the power of this inversion. For once, field performance was not filtered through layers of management. It was recognized where it originated. Representatives were not thanked collectively; they were named individually. Achievement was specific. Praise was earned.

The impact was immediate and lasting. Those who stood on that stage returned not merely encouraged, but changed. They carried a sense of legitimacy that no memo could confer. They had been seen—not as instruments of execution, but as professionals worthy of respect.

The Srinagar milestone also reshaped aspiration. Stories traveled faster than circulars ever could. In territories far from the venue, representatives recalibrated their ambitions. Excellence no longer felt abstract. It had a location, a memory, a moment.

For Gupta, Srinagar marked the maturation of a philosophy he held deeply: that recognition, when done right, elevates behavior without cheapening it. By placing the field at the center of the ceremony and leadership at the periphery, he reinforced a simple truth—that organizations succeed not because of titles at the top, but because of discipline and dignity at the front lines.

The Srinagar milestone endures as an example of how culture is shaped through deliberate acts. It was not the geography that mattered, but the gesture. And in that gesture, Tarun Gupta once again demonstrated his rare understanding of how respect, once conferred authentically, becomes a force multiplier for excellence.

Why Incentives Started Only at 101%

To Tarun Gupta, incentives were never meant to compensate effort. Effort, he believed, was the price of entry. Incentives existed for a different purpose: to mark distinction. This belief lay at the heart of his insistence that rewards begin not at achievement, but beyond it—at 101 percent.

The logic was deliberately uncompromising. Targets, Gupta argued, are commitments, not aspirations. They represent the minimum performance the organization has already paid for—through salary, training, and trust. To reward someone for meeting a target, in his view, was to confuse obligation with excellence.

By setting the threshold at 101 percent, Gupta drew a clear line. A performance of up to 100 percent was expected. Performance beyond it was exceptional. The distinction mattered because it preserved the meaning of achievement. Incentives, once diluted, lose their power to inspire.

This approach also protected the culture from complacency. When incentives begin too early, effort plateaus. People learn to optimize for reward rather than growth. Gupta wanted the opposite. He wanted momentum—an organizational habit of pushing past comfort.

The policy was not popular at first. Some saw it as harsh. Others worried it would demotivate average performers. Gupta disagreed. He believed clarity was kinder than ambiguity. When standards are explicit, disappointment is informative, not personal.

Importantly, the 101 percent rule was paired with dignity. Those who did not qualify were not shamed. Their performance was acknowledged as satisfactory. The absence of reward was not a penalty; it was a signal. The system encouraged aspiration without creating resentment.

Over time, the rule reshaped behavior. Representatives began to think in margins rather than thresholds. Managers coached differently. Conversations shifted from Did you hit the target? to How far beyond did you go?

For Gupta, incentives were a language. By speaking in 101 percent, he told the organization what it valued—not effort alone, but excellence. The rule endured because it was fair, transparent, and consistent.

In setting incentives beyond the expected, Tarun Gupta reaffirmed a core belief: that excellence must be unmistakably distinguished from adequacy—and that when recognition is reserved for those who cross that line, it retains the power to inspire.

Chapter 13

Building Intellectual Giants

Intelligence Must Be Cultivated, Not Assumed

Tarun Gupta never assumed that intelligence was a fixed trait. He treated it as a capacity that could be expanded—or allowed to stagnate—by design.

In his view, professional growth did not come from experience alone. Experience, unexamined, merely reinforced habit. What mattered was exposure—to new ideas, unfamiliar frameworks, and ways of thinking that unsettled certainty. This is why Gupta deliberately brought global thinkers, researchers, and marketing scholars into dialogue with field managers and brand teams.

The objective was not imitation. It was a stretch.

By encouraging managers to engage with ideas beyond their immediate context, Gupta raised the quality of internal conversations. Questions became sharper. Assumptions were challenged. Marketing ceased to be a set of tactics and became a discipline of thought.

The Glaxo Marketing Journal served the same purpose. Writing, Gupta believed, was a test of clarity. If an idea could not be articulated simply, it was not yet understood. Intellectual rigor, like executional discipline, had to be practiced.

The principle was uncompromising:

Organizations grow intellectually only when they deliberately invest in thinking, not just doing.

For Gupta, building intellectual giants was not about brilliance.

It was about creating an environment in which curiosity was expected and complacency was unacceptable.

Tarun Gupta was not content to build competent managers. Competence, he believed, stabilized organizations but did not elevate them. What he sought instead were intellectual giants—leaders capable of thinking beyond immediate tasks, questioning assumptions, and navigating complexity with confidence. Chapter 13 explores how he set about cultivating such minds.

Gupta held a firm conviction: intellectual growth is not a by-product of experience; it is a deliberate pursuit. Left to their own devices, even talented managers plateau. To prevent this, he created an environment in which curiosity was expected, and ignorance was temporary. Reading, discussion, and debate were not optional extras—they were part of the job.

One of his most distinctive moves was to bring the world into the organization. Gupta invited leading thinkers—Sidney Levy, Gerald Zaltman, John Little, and others—to interact with managers who might otherwise never encounter such ideas. These were not ceremonial lectures. They were working sessions. Managers were expected to listen actively, question respectfully, and reflect critically.

Gupta's aim was not imitation, but expansion. He wanted his teams to see marketing as a discipline with depth and lineage, not a collection of tricks. Exposure to global thinking reframed local problems. Familiar challenges appeared newly complex—and newly solvable.

This intellectual ambition extended to internal platforms such as the Glaxo Marketing Journal, which Gupta encouraged as a forum for serious thought. Articles were curated for relevance, not fashion. Concepts were debated, not adopted uncritically. Managers learned to articulate ideas in writing, sharpening thought through expression.

Gupta also modeled the behavior he demanded. He read voraciously. He questioned relentlessly. He changed his mind when evidence warranted it. Intellectual authority, he believed, came not from certainty, but from engagement.

Importantly, Gupta distinguished intellectual rigor from academic abstraction. Ideas had to earn their place through applicability. Managers were encouraged to ask, What does this change tomorrow? Theory that could not inform action was set aside.

Building intellectual giants was, in Gupta's mind, an investment in resilience. Markets change. Products age. Strategies expire. But leaders trained to think critically adapt. They ask better questions, make fewer assumptions, and recover faster from error.

In cultivating such minds, Tarun Gupta ensured that his influence extended beyond systems and structures. He left behind a generation of leaders equipped not just with tools, but with frameworks of thought—capable of carrying his legacy forward in an industry that would continue to evolve.

Vignette: Bringing the World to Glaxo

Levy, Zaltman, John Little — and Beyond

Tarun Gupta never believed that intellectual growth could occur in isolation. For managers to think differently, he felt, they needed to encounter ideas that unsettled familiarity. The most efficient way to do that was to bring the world to them.

At Glaxo, this took the form of conversations that were unprecedented for the time. Thinkers such as Sidney Levy, who had articulated the idea of brands as symbols and meaning systems; Gerald Zaltman, whose work explored the subconscious dimensions of consumer thought; and John Little, a pioneer of marketing science and modeling, were introduced not as distant authorities, but as interlocutors.

These encounters were not ceremonial lectures delivered to passive audiences. Gupta designed them as engagements. Managers were expected to prepare, to question, and to connect abstract ideas to lived practice. The goal was not admiration, but application.

Levy's discussions challenged managers to see brands not merely as products, but as carriers of meaning—an idea that resonated deeply in pharmaceutical marketing, where trust and belief are as critical as efficacy. Zaltman's explorations of mental models pushed teams to recognize that decision-making is rarely linear, even among physicians. Little's analytical frameworks brought rigor to intuition, showing how data could sharpen rather than stifle judgment.

What made these sessions transformative was context. Gupta did not import ideas wholesale. He curated them. Each thinker was chosen because their work illuminated a real problem the organization faced. Global theory was filtered through local reality.

The effect on Glaxo's managers was profound. They began to see their work as part of a larger intellectual tradition. Vocabulary expanded.

Questions deepened. Marketing conversations moved beyond tactics into philosophy and systems.

Gupta's own role in these interactions was revealing. He did not position himself as a gatekeeper of knowledge. He participated as a learner, probing and challenging alongside his teams. In doing so, he modeled the very behavior he sought to cultivate.

Bringing the world to Glaxo was not about prestige. It was about perspective. Gupta understood that leaders who never encounter ideas beyond their immediate environment eventually confuse familiarity with truth.

This vignette captures a defining aspect of Tarun Gupta's legacy: his insistence that Indian pharmaceutical marketing deserved—and could sustain—global intellectual engagement. By opening windows to the world, he ensured that his teams did not merely execute well, but thought boldly and deeply, long before such expectations became commonplace.

The Glaxo Marketing Journal

Expanding Mental Horizons

Tarun Gupta believed that thinking improves when it is made visible. Conversations sharpen ideas in the moment, but writing forces discipline over time. The Glaxo Marketing Journal emerged from this conviction—not as a corporate newsletter, but as an intellectual instrument designed to stretch the organization's collective mind.

At a time when internal communication was largely transactional, the Journal set a different tone. It was not meant to announce targets or celebrate quarterly wins. It existed to provoke thought. Articles were chosen not for immediacy, but for relevance—ideas that challenged assumptions, reframed problems, and introduced unfamiliar perspectives.

Gupta was personally involved in its curation. He treated content selection as a strategic act. Academic papers, global case studies, and essays by leading thinkers were distilled and contextualized. The Journal was not about showcasing erudition; it was about accessibility. Complex ideas were translated into language that managers could engage with and debate.

What distinguished the Journal was its expectation of participation. Readers were not passive consumers. Managers were encouraged to respond, question, and contribute. Writing became a form of leadership. Those who could articulate thought clearly earned intellectual authority, regardless of title.

The Journal also served as a bridge between theory and practice. Articles were discussed in meetings, referenced in planning sessions, and applied in the field. Concepts did not remain abstract; they were tested, adapted, and sometimes discarded. Learning became iterative.

Over time, the Journal's presence altered the organization's rhythm. Reading became habitual. Discussion deepened. Managers began to see themselves not just as executors of plans, but as thinkers engaged in an evolving discipline.

Gupta understood that organizations stagnate when their ideas do. By institutionalizing a platform for reflection, he ensured that curiosity remained alive even as systems matured. The Journal became a quiet counterweight to routine—a reminder that excellence requires continual renewal of thought.

In expanding mental horizons through the Glaxo Marketing Journal, Tarun Gupta demonstrated a rare insight: that intellectual culture is built not through grand gestures, but through sustained exposure to ideas—and the expectation that those ideas will be engaged with seriously.

Part V

Integrity, Philosophy, and Academic Legacy

Integrity is a System, Not a Sentiment

Tarun Gupta did not treat integrity as a personal virtue to be admired. He treated it as an organizational condition to be designed.

In his experience, ethical lapses rarely arose from malice. They emerged from ambiguity—unclear rules, mixed signals, tolerated shortcuts. Where systems were vague, judgment eroded. Where incentives were misaligned, rationalization flourished.

Gupta's response was characteristically practical. He removed discretion where discretion invited abuse. He clarified processes where informality bred distortion. Integrity, in his world, was not enforced through exhortation but through structure.

This philosophy extended beyond corporate life into the classroom. As a teacher, Gupta resisted abstraction and moral posturing. He believed ethics could not be memorized; they had to be practiced under constraint. Students were challenged with live cases, incomplete information, and real consequences—conditions under which values revealed themselves.

The Unifying belief was Simple and Demanding

When integrity is left to intention, it weakens; when it is built into systems, it endures.

Part V explores this conviction across roles—leader, teacher, and guide—and traces how TG's insistence on clarity outlived the positions he once held.

As Tarun Gupta's influence expanded, something about his leadership became increasingly clear: his authority did not rest solely on results. Many executives deliver growth. Few shape character. Fewer still leave behind a philosophy that endures after titles recede. Part V turns to the inner architecture of Gupta's legacy—the values, beliefs, and teaching instincts that governed how he led and why others followed.

For Gupta, integrity was not a personal virtue to be admired in isolation. It was a system to be designed. He distrusted moral exhortation unsupported by structure. Ethical behavior, he believed, flourished when processes made the right action the easiest one. This belief would later manifest in precise audits, transparent reimbursements, and the elimination of practices that quietly eroded self-respect in the field.

Yet integrity alone did not explain Gupta's impact. Beneath his decisions lay a coherent philosophy of management—one that balanced rigor with humanity, discipline with dignity. He believed people rose to the expectations placed upon them when those expectations were clear, fair, and consistently enforced. Standards were not negotiable, but individuals were respected.

This part of the book also traces Gupta's transition from corporate leadership to academic influence—not as a retreat, but as a continuation. In classrooms at institutions such as JBIMS and NMIMS, he brought the same insistence on clarity and practice that had defined his corporate career. Textbooks gave way to live cases. Theory was interrogated through reality. Students were unsettled, then transformed.

Gupta did not see himself as an academic in the traditional sense. He saw himself as a teacher of judgment. His classrooms were extensions of the field—places where ideas were tested against consequence. Education, for him, was not about transmitting knowledge but about shaping how future leaders would think when certainty was absent.

Part V explores how integrity, philosophy, and teaching converged into a single legacy. It reveals a leader who understood that systems outlive strategies, and that values, when operationalized, become culture.

In examining this dimension of Tarun Gupta's life, the narrative shifts from what he built to why it endured—and how his deepest influence was felt not in balance sheets, but in the minds and conduct of those who learned under him.

Chapter 14

The Teacher, Philosopher, and Guide

"I Am Here to Teach the Practice"

In classrooms where students expected frameworks, Tarun Gupta delivered reality.

He rejected textbook cases in favor of live brands, live markets, and live consequences. Students were unsettled—and transformed.

Years later, many would realize that he was not teaching marketing at all. He was teaching how to think in the face of uncertainty.

Tarun Gupta did not retire into teaching. He extended himself into it. When he stepped into classrooms at institutions such as the Jamnalal Bajaj Institute of Management Studies (JBIMS) and later NMIMS, he brought not the detachment of an academic but the urgency of a practitioner who had lived with the consequences of his decisions. For Gupta, teaching was not a change of role; it was a change of audience.

Students who expected frameworks were often surprised by his opening question: What actually happened? Gupta had little patience for abstraction unmoored from reality. He believed that management could not be understood in theory alone—it had to be confronted in context, under pressure, with incomplete information. His classes reflected this belief.

Textbooks, when they appeared at all, were supporting actors. The main text was the market itself. Gupta brought current issues from the Business World, live brand challenges, and unfolding industry shifts into the classroom. Students were not asked to admire success after the fact; they were asked to diagnose problems before outcomes were known. Uncertainty was not avoided—it was central to the lesson.

Gupta's teaching style was demanding, sometimes unsettling. He challenged students to defend their thinking, not their vocabulary. Fluency without judgment did not impress him. Silence, when thoughtful, was respected. He was not interested in answers that sounded correct; he wanted answers that could survive reality.

Yet beneath the rigor lay a deep generosity. Gupta took students seriously. He believed that potential revealed itself when expectations were high and guidance was firm. Many who struggled initially found their footing not because the material became easier, but because they learned how to think.

Outside the classroom, Gupta served as a guide in the truest sense. Former students sought him out years later, not for technical advice, but for perspective. He listened carefully, spoke sparingly, and framed problems in ways that restored clarity. His counsel was rarely prescriptive. Instead, it illuminated trade-offs and consequences.

What distinguished Gupta as a teacher was his refusal to separate ethics from effectiveness. Decisions, he insisted, carried moral weight. Integrity was not an abstract principle; it was a daily practice. Students learned that leadership demanded not only intelligence but also courage.

In this role—as teacher, philosopher, and guide—Tarun Gupta reached perhaps his widest audience. His influence extended beyond organizations into generations of managers who carried his thinking into diverse domains. He did not seek disciples. He cultivated thinkers.

Chapter 14 captures this final evolution of his career—not as a winding down, but as a distillation. In the classroom, as in the corporation, Gupta's enduring lesson remained the same: that management is not about control, but about judgment—and that judgment, once learned, shapes a lifetime.

JBIMS and NMIMS

From Corporate Leader to Academic Mentor

When Tarun Gupta entered the classrooms of JBIMS and later NMIMS, he did not arrive as a visiting executive dispensing war stories. He arrived as a practitioner intent on reshaping how management itself was understood. For Gupta, the move from corporate leadership to academia was not a retreat from relevance; it was a conscious shift toward a deeper kind of influence.

At JBIMS, an institution known for its intellectual rigor and debate, Gupta found an audience eager for theory—and he responded by complicating it. He challenged students to test every concept against lived experience. Frameworks were welcomed, but only as starting points. The real work began when assumptions collided with reality.

Gupta's classes quickly developed a reputation. They were intense, unscripted, and demanding. Students were expected to engage actively, to read widely, and to think independently. There were no safe answers. A well-phrased response without substance was dismantled gently but decisively. What mattered was not confidence, but clarity.

When he later moved to NMIMS, Gupta carried the same philosophy with him, adapting it to a broader and increasingly diverse cohort. Here, too, he resisted the comfort of predictability. He brought current business issues into the classroom, often unfolding in real time. Students learned to reason without the reassurance of hindsight.

Across both institutions, Gupta saw education as preparation for uncertainty. He believed that the true value of a management program lay not in placement statistics, but in the quality of judgment its graduates displayed when conditions were ambiguous and stakes were high.

Gupta's mentorship extended beyond scheduled lectures. Students sought him out for guidance on careers, ethical dilemmas, and leadership challenges. He listened carefully, framing advice not as instruction, but as perspective. His role was not to decide for them, but to sharpen their decision-making.

What distinguished Gupta as an academic mentor was his insistence on practice. He famously declared, “I am here to teach the practice.” It was not a dismissal of theory, but a demand that theory earn its place. Knowledge, he believed, achieved dignity only when it could be acted upon responsibly.

In bridging JBIMS and NMIMS, Tarun Gupta built a continuum between corporate reality and academic inquiry. He showed students that management was neither an abstract science nor a set of tricks, but a discipline grounded in judgment, ethics, and consequence.

This chapter traces that journey—from boardrooms to classrooms—not as a change in identity, but as its refinement. In becoming an academic mentor, Gupta extended his legacy from organizations to minds, ensuring that his influence would continue long after his direct authority had ended.

Vignette: "I Am Here to Teach the Practice"

The statement was delivered without flourish, almost casually, yet it altered the temperature of the room. "I am here to teach the practice." For students accustomed to lectures anchored in models and examinations, the words landed as both a challenge and a promise.

Tarun Gupta did not dismiss the theory. He simply refused to privilege it. In his classrooms, theory was invited to speak—but only after it had proven its relevance. Students quickly learned that citing frameworks without understanding their consequences was not an achievement. It was an evasion.

The vignette that would become legend began with a familiar ritual. A student confidently presented a textbook answer, well-structured and fluent. Gupta listened attentively, then paused. "What would you do on Monday morning?" he asked. The room fell quiet. The answer, perfectly acceptable on paper, dissolved under the weight of reality.

Gupta's insistence on practice was not a rejection of intellect; it was a defense of it. He believed that thinking reached maturity only when it confronted uncertainty. In his hands, the classroom became a rehearsal space for decision-making under pressure.

He brought live cases into discussion—brands in flux, organizations mid-transition, markets shifting unpredictably. There were no correct answers, only better questions. Students learned to reason aloud, revise assumptions, and accept ambiguity without paralysis.

The phrase "teach the practice" came to embody Gupta's pedagogical philosophy. It meant learning to observe before judging, to listen before prescribing, and to act with awareness of consequence. Ethics were not an appendix; they were integral to every decision discussed.

Over time, students began to understand what Gupta was offering. He was not training them to pass exams. He was preparing them to face moments when guidance would be absent and responsibility unavoidable.

The vignette endures because it captures Gupta at his most distilled. In a single sentence, he articulated a lifetime of belief: that management is not mastered in abstraction, but earned through engagement with reality—and that the true role of a teacher is not to provide answers, but to cultivate judgment.

In declaring that he was there to teach the practice, Tarun Gupta reminded generations of students that education, at its best, is not about knowing more—but about choosing better.

Experiential Learning

Live Cases as Textbooks

Tarun Gupta believed that learning detached from consequence was incomplete. Textbooks, he felt, offered clarity without risk—answers already stabilized by hindsight. Useful, but insufficient. If managers were to develop judgment, they needed to think in situations where outcomes were uncertain and responsibility was real. This conviction shaped his commitment to experiential learning, where live cases replaced textbooks as the primary medium of instruction.

In Gupta's classrooms, the "case" was not a neatly packaged narrative with a known ending. It was a situation unfolding in real time—an industry in transition, a brand under pressure, a leadership dilemma unresolved. Students were asked to engage before the story concluded, when information was partial, and choices carried weight.

This approach unsettled many at first. Without the comfort of precedent, students struggled. They searched for the "right" answer, only to discover that none existed. Gupta welcomed this discomfort. He believed it mirrored the conditions under which real managers operate. Learning, in his view, occurred not in certainty but in navigation.

Live cases demanded a different kind of preparation. Students had to read widely, observe closely, and connect disparate signals. They learned to identify what mattered amid noise. Gupta insisted that analysis be grounded in action: What would you do? Why? What are the consequences?

Importantly, experiential learning also brought ethics to the foreground. Decisions could not be evaluated purely on efficiency or profitability. Students were asked to consider trust, fairness, and long-term impact. Values were not discussed as abstract ideals, but as practical constraints.

Gupta's role in these sessions was that of a guide, not a judge. He listened carefully, challenged assumptions, and reframed questions. When discussions drifted into abstraction, he returned them to practice. Who decides? When? With what information? These questions anchored thought.

Over time, students began to appreciate the power of this method. They learned not just how to analyze, but how to decide. They developed confidence not from certainty, but from process.

By treating live cases as textbooks, Tarun Gupta inverted the traditional classroom hierarchy. Reality became the teacher. The classroom became a laboratory for judgment. And students left not with answers memorized, but with habits of thinking that would serve them long after specific theories faded.

In embracing experiential learning, Gupta affirmed his enduring belief: that education achieves its highest purpose not when it transmits knowledge, but when it prepares individuals to act wisely in the face of uncertainty.

Chapter 15

The 10-Year Training Marathon

Training Is a Commitment, Not an Event

Tarun Gupta rejected the idea that training was a reward for retention or a privilege reserved for high performers. To him, training was a responsibility of leadership—owed to the role, not negotiated as part of tenure.

In an industry where attrition was often cited as a reason to limit investment, Gupta took the opposite view. He believed that withholding training weakened the system itself. People might leave, but the standards they carried would remain. Training, therefore, was not a cost to be minimized; it was infrastructure.

This belief shaped what came to be known as the ten-year training marathon. Learning was continuous, repetitive, and cumulative. Concepts were revisited. Skills were reinforced. Judgment was sharpened over time. There was no graduation ceremony—only higher expectations.

Gupta understood that capability decays when it is treated episodically. Knowledge fades. Habits soften. Discipline erodes. Only sustained practice kept the organization intellectually fit.

The principle he insisted upon was demanding but clear:

Organizations that train intermittently develop skills; organizations that train continuously build professions.

For Gupta, the true measure of training was not retention.

It was whether standards survived people.

Tarun Gupta viewed training not as an event, but as a responsibility. Many organizations invested heavily in induction programs, annual workshops, and motivational off-sites—only to accept attrition as an inevitable loss. Gupta rejected this logic entirely. If people left, he believed, the organization still carried an obligation to have trained them well. Knowledge, once imparted, did not vanish with resignation; it flowed outward, shaping the industry.

The 10-year training marathon emerged from this belief. It was not branded as such at the time, nor announced with fanfare. It unfolded gradually, sustained by Gupta's conviction that learning had to be continuous, cumulative, and uncompromising.

Year after year, training programs were designed not to refresh memory, but to deepen capability. Concepts returned at higher levels of sophistication. Field techniques were revisited with greater rigor. Managers were exposed repeatedly to strategy, ethics, and execution—until these became reflex rather than recollection.

Gupta resisted the temptation to tailor training only for retention. Attrition, he accepted, was part of organizational life. But dilution of standards was not. Even if individuals left, the discipline they carried with them would raise the industry's baseline. In this sense, Gupta's training philosophy was expansive rather than defensive.

The programs themselves were demanding. Attendance was expected. Preparation was required. Participation was active. Gupta believed that seriousness signaled respect. Training was not entertainment; it was an investment.

Over time, the marathon produced leaders who shared a common grammar of management. They thought in systems. They valued clarity. They understood that performance was not accidental. This shared intellectual foundation allowed ideas to travel seamlessly across roles and organizations.

The endurance of the marathon lay in its consistency. Gupta did not abandon training when budgets tightened or results improved. He believed that success was precisely when complacency was most dangerous.

In sustaining a decade-long commitment to training, Tarun Gupta demonstrated a long view rarely seen in corporate life. He was not building for quarters or even careers. He was building capacity.

The 10-year training marathon stands as a testament to Gupta's belief that excellence is cultivated, not accelerated, and that the true measure of training is not how long people stay, but how deeply they think wherever they go.

Vignette: Braving the Downpour

The Lonavala Drive

The rain that morning was not symbolic. It was relentless, unyielding, and plainly dangerous. Roads disappeared beneath sheets of water. Visibility collapsed. Advisers urged a delay. Reason suggested cancellation. Yet Tarun Gupta got into the car.

A training session had been scheduled in Lonavala. Participants had traveled. Commitments had been made. For Gupta, that was sufficient. Training, he believed, was not conditional on convenience. It was a promise.

The drive was slow and tense. The wipers strained against the downpour. Traffic thinned, then stalled. At points, turning back would have been the sensible choice. Gupta did not dramatize the decision. He simply proceeded.

When he arrived—late, wet, and visibly exhausted—the room fell silent. No announcement was needed. The message had already been delivered.

Gupta did not speak about the journey. He began the session as planned. The material was demanding. The discussion was rigorous. The standards were unchanged. That, too, was deliberate. The effort expended to be present did not excuse anyone from the effort required to learn.

The vignette endured because it revealed something essential about Gupta's leadership. He did not ask others to value training. He showed them how. By honoring the commitment under difficult conditions, he removed any doubt about its importance.

Years later, participants would recall not the slides or the exercises, but the arrival. It reframed their understanding of discipline. Training was no longer an optional activity to be postponed when circumstances intervened. It was a priority that held even in adverse conditions.

Braving the downpour was not an act of bravado. It was an act of coherence. Gupta's words and actions aligned. In doing so, he taught a lesson more durable than any curriculum: that leadership is revealed not in what is postponed, but in what is honored.

The Lonavala drive became part of institutional memory because it captured Gupta's philosophy in motion—quiet, resolute, and uncompromising in its respect for commitment.

The "Un-Unilever" Philosophy of Continuous Training

Tarun Gupta admired organizations like Unilever. He understood their discipline, their rigor, and their extraordinary commitment to leadership development. Unilever trained deeply, systematically, and early—identifying potential, investing heavily, and accepting that not everyone so trained would remain. It was a model built on selection and scale, and it worked.

Gupta did not reject this model. He chose to depart from it.

Where organizations like Unilever concentrated training on future leaders, Gupta believed training was a responsibility attached to the role itself. Anyone entrusted with influencing doctors, patients, or brands deserved continuous development—not because they might rise, but because they already mattered.

This belief shaped what would later be described as his "Un-Unilever" philosophy.

Training, under Gupta, did not peak early and then taper. It deepened with time. Field representatives were retrained year after year. Managers returned repeatedly to the same ideas, each time with greater sophistication. Learning was not accelerated for the promising and was reduced for the rest. It was sustained for all.

Attrition did not weaken this conviction. Gupta accepted that people would leave. What he refused to accept was under-preparing those who stayed—or those who might someday lead elsewhere. If trained people carried discipline, ethics, and clarity into the wider industry, that was not leakage. It was leadership.

This philosophy required courage. Budgets had to be defended without the comfort of retention guarantees. Cynicism had to be ignored. Gupta persisted because he believed something fundamental: professional dignity depends on preparation.

In choosing continuity over selectivity, Gupta took the longer view. He was not merely developing talent for one company. He was raising the standard of pharmaceutical marketing itself.

The "Un-Unilever" philosophy was never about being anti-corporate or anti-system. It was about being pro-responsibility. And in that choice, Tarun Gupta revealed a defining feature of his leadership: the belief that training, when done seriously, outlives organizations—and that the true measure of development is not who stays, but how people think wherever they go.

Chapter 16

Integrity and the Outsider Mindset

Integrity as a System, Not a Sermon

Gupta did not moralize integrity. He operationalized it.

Whether through point-to-point audits or cultural resets, he designed systems where ethical behavior was the easiest path—not the hardest choice.

For him, integrity was not character alone. It was architecture.

Tarun Gupta never fully belonged to the systems he transformed—and that was precisely his strength. He cultivated what might best be described as an outsider mindset: a deliberate distance from conventions that had normalized compromise. From this vantage point, practices others accepted as inevitable appeared, to him, as choices—and therefore subject to change.

Integrity, in Gupta's framework, was not a private virtue. It was an operational stance. He was wary of moral posturing unaccompanied by structure, and equally wary of structures that quietly incentivized ethical drift. To address this, he set about redesigning systems so that integrity was not heroic—but routine.

Small practices mattered. Expense claims, for instance, were treated not as minor administrative details but as reflections of character. Gupta introduced point-to-point audits that removed ambiguity from reimbursements. There would be no padding, no informal allowances, no quiet indulgences. The rules were clear, and so were the expectations. In eliminating discretion, he eliminated temptation.

Another entrenched practice Gupta confronted was the culture of alcohol-fueled camaraderie. Drinking, often framed as bonding, had become an unspoken requirement in some professional settings. Gupta saw something else: erosion of self-respect. He replaced whiskey with soft drinks—not as a moral judgment, but as a professional reset. Work, he believed, did not require intoxication to build trust.

What made these interventions effective was their consistency. Gupta did not single out individuals or dramatize enforcement. He altered the environment. Ethical behavior became the path of least resistance. Deviations stood out not because they were punished, but because they no longer fit.

The outsider mindset allowed Gupta to question what insiders no longer saw. He asked why practices existed, not how long they had endured. When answers defaulted to tradition, he acted.

This approach earned him respect, and occasionally resentment. Yet Gupta was unmoved. He believed that leadership demanded the courage to stand apart from convenience. Once compromised, integrity was difficult to restore.

Chapter 16 reveals the quiet rigor with which Tarun Gupta aligned values and systems. By remaining an outsider—even at the center—he preserved the clarity needed to confront ethical erosion. In doing so, he demonstrated that the most enduring reforms are not loud or punitive, but structural—and that integrity, when designed into systems, becomes culture.

Ending the Taxi-Fare Malpractice

For Tarun Gupta, ethical decay rarely announced itself in dramatic scandals. It crept in quietly, normalized through small concessions that seemed harmless in isolation. The taxi-fare malpractice was one such concession—widely practiced, rarely questioned, and tacitly accepted as part of the system. Gupta saw it differently. To him, it was not a minor irregularity. It was a fracture in self-respect.

The practice was simple and insidious. Expense claims were rounded up. Distances were inflated. Receipts were adjusted. No one spoke of dishonesty; it was framed as entitlement, compensation for inconvenience, or an unspoken perk of the role. Over time, the behavior lost its ethical charge. It became routine.

Gupta intervened not with accusation, but with design. He introduced point-to-point audits that eliminated ambiguity. Travel was reimbursed strictly from origin to destination, in a verifiable, transparent manner. There would be no room for interpretation—and therefore no room for rationalization.

The change unsettled many. What had once been invisible was now exposed. Some resisted quietly; others argued practicality. Gupta listened, but he did not relent. He believed that organizations betray their people when they allow small dishonesty to masquerade as necessity.

What followed was not demoralization, but relief. With clarity came dignity. Representatives no longer had to navigate moral gray zones. Managers no longer had to look away. The system, once complicit, now supported integrity.

Gupta understood that character is shaped as much by environment as by intention. By removing the incentive—and the excuse—for malpractice, he restored a sense of professional pride. People were paid for their work, not their cunning.

Ending the taxi-fare malpractice was emblematic of Gupta's leadership. He did not preach ethics. He engineered them. In doing so, he demonstrated that integrity does not require heroism—only clarity, consistency, and the courage to remove what corrodes trust.

It was a small reform with a large effect, reinforcing a principle Gupta held deeply: that when organizations protect self-respect, they strengthen not just compliance, but character.

Confronting the Drinking Culture

In many corporate environments, drinking had come to be seen as a social lubricant—an unspoken expectation at meetings, off-sites, and celebrations. It was framed as camaraderie, a way to flatten hierarchy and build bonds. Tarun Gupta saw something else. To him, the drinking culture represented a quiet erosion of professionalism, one that blurred boundaries and diluted self-respect.

Gupta did not approach the issue as a moral crusader. He was not interested in judging personal choices. His concern lay with what the culture required. When participation in alcohol-centered rituals became a proxy for belonging, those who abstained—by choice, belief, or circumstance—were subtly marginalized. Professional engagement should never demand personal compromise.

His response was characteristically structural. Gupta removed alcohol from official settings and replaced it with simple alternatives—soft drinks, tea, and conversation. The change was understated, almost anticlimactic. There were no speeches, no policies circulated with fanfare. The environment shifted quietly, and with it, expectations.

Predictably, there was initial discomfort. Some worried that informality would suffer, that relationships would weaken. The opposite occurred. Conversations became clearer. Boundaries sharpened. Respect increased. Work-related dialogue no longer competed with intoxication for attention.

Gupta understood that culture is shaped by defaults. By changing what was normal, he changed what was acceptable. Professional interaction no longer requires chemical assistance. Presence, preparation, and mutual regard were sufficient.

The deeper impact was psychological. Employees began to feel that the organization valued their contributions, not their conformity. The field, in particular, experienced this as a restoration of dignity. Work was work. Socializing was optional. The distinction mattered.

Confronting the drinking culture was not about abstinence. It was about autonomy. Gupta believed that leadership should expand freedom, not narrow it. By dismantling a practice that subtly coerced participation, he reaffirmed a principle that ran through all his reforms: self-respect is foundational to performance.

In addressing this issue without drama or denunciation, Tarun Gupta once again demonstrated his instinct for ethical design. He did not shame behavior; he changed context. And in doing so, he showed that professionalism, when thoughtfully protected, becomes not a constraint—but a source of quiet strength.

Chapter 17: The Legacy of "TG"

Chapter 18: Lessons from the Road not Taken

Part VI

The Lasting Impact

When a Man becomes a Movement

Long after Tarun Gupta stepped away from corporate roles, his influence continued—through students, protégés, and systems that outlived him.

Tributes following his passing spoke less about the positions he held and more about the minds he shaped. In that distinction lies the measure of his legacy.

Some legacies announce themselves through monuments and titles. Others reveal themselves more quietly—through habits that persist, standards that endure, and ways of thinking that outlive the individual who first articulated them. Tarun Gupta's legacy belongs to the latter kind. By the time he stepped away from formal authority, his influence had already escaped institutional boundaries.

Part VI examines what remained after Tarun Gupta left the room.

By the late 1970s, an extraordinary pattern had taken shape across the Indian pharmaceutical industry. Former Glaxo marketing executives—trained under Gupta's discipline—had dispersed into competing organizations, carrying with them a shared grammar of management. At one point, it was estimated that more than half of the industry's marketing activity was being led by professionals shaped by this system. No mandate had enforced this. No consolidation had engineered it. The influence had spread organically.

This diffusion mattered because it was intellectual, not positional. Gupta did not leave behind a centralized doctrine or a network bound by loyalty. He left behind habits of clarity, respect for execution, and intolerance for ambiguity. Companies that had never worked with him began to resemble one another—not by design, but by adoption.

The impact extended beyond structure into ethos. Product management matured. Field discipline strengthened. Data replaced anecdote. Training became continuous rather than episodic. Integrity was operationalized. What had once been exceptional became expected.

Part VI explores how this influence manifested—through protégés who rose to leadership, through decisions that echoed his principles, and through missed opportunities that revealed his long view. It also examines the humility that underpinned his philosophy: the belief that leaders must remain students, and that learning never ends.

This final section is not an epilogue. It is an accounting. It asks what it means to shape an industry without owning it, to teach without prescribing, and to lead without insisting on permanence.

In tracing Tarun Gupta's lasting impact, the narrative returns to its central insight: that the most powerful legacies are not built by control, but by cultivation—and that when ideas are designed to travel, they do.

Chapter 17

The Legacy of "TG"

Legacy is Measured by what Continues without You

Tarun Gupta never spoke of legacy. He spoke of standards.

In his view, leadership was successful only when it became unnecessary—when systems functioned, judgments held, and discipline persisted in the leader's absence. Influence that required constant reinforcement was fragile. Influence embedded in people and process endured.

By the late 1970s, the evidence of this approach had become visible across the Indian pharmaceutical industry. Former Glaxo managers trained under TG's system went on to lead marketing functions in competing companies. They differed in strategy and style, but shared a common grammar of thinking. Without coordination or allegiance, a quiet consistency emerged.

This was not a Replication, It was a Transfer

TG's influence spread not through authority, but through capability. Those who learned under him carried his insistence on clarity, discipline, and judgment into new contexts. They adapted methods, but retained standards.

The Enduring Lesson was Subtle but Powerful

A leader's true legacy is not what he builds, but what others are able to build after him.

In this sense, TG left no organization behind.

He left behind a profession better able to sustain itself.

By the late 1970s, an extraordinary pattern had quietly taken shape—one that no organizational chart could explain.

Across companies, portfolios, and competing boardrooms, former Glaxo marketing executives began to surface with striking regularity. They were not aligned by allegiance, but by philosophy. They spoke thc same language of clarity, discipline, and systems. They asked the same questions. They made decisions that felt uncannily familiar.

At one point, it was estimated that more than fifty percent of the marketing activity of the entire Indian pharmaceutical industry was being managed by professionals who had trained under the Glaxo system.

This was not Consolidation, It was Diffusion

Tarun Gupta did not build an empire. He built a way of thinking that traveled—portable, replicable, and resilient. His influence did not reside in market share or corporate dominance, but in the mental models carried by those who had learned under him and then moved on.

Competitors unknowingly adopted Glaxo's discipline. Field structures across companies began to resemble one another. Product management, once tentative, became authoritative. Data, once peripheral, became central.

The Industry had not Copied a Company, It had Absorbed a Philosophy

This is the rarest form of leadership impact: when ideas outgrow institutions, and a teacher's presence is felt most strongly where his name is no longer visible.

Legacies are often measured in tenure, titles, or the scale of organizations led. Tarun Gupta's legacy resists such accounting. It is not anchored in a single company or role, but in a way of thinking that became embedded across an entire industry. By the time his formal career receded from view, his influence had already multiplied—carried forward by those who had learned under him and then moved on.

What distinguished Gupta's legacy was its diffusive quality. He did not build a following bound by allegiance. He built capability. Former colleagues and students dispersed into competing firms, consulting roles, academia, and leadership positions. They did not replicate Glaxo. They replicated discipline.

By the late 1970s, this diffusion had reached a remarkable scale. At one point, it was estimated that more than fifty percent of the marketing activity of the Indian pharmaceutical industry was being managed by professionals who had trained under the Glaxo marketing system during Gupta's tenure. No strategic plan had aimed for this outcome. It emerged organically, as trained managers carried a shared grammar of strategy, execution, and integrity into new environments.

This was not Influenced through Control, It was Influenced by Standards

Across companies, familiar patterns began to appear. Product management took on real authority. Visual aids became narratives rather than catalogues. Field execution was professionalized. Prescription data informed strategy. Training was treated as continuous rather than episodic. Integrity was designed into systems rather than asserted rhetorically.

Gupta's protégés did not agree on everything. They argued, adapted, and evolved. But they recognized one another instantly. The questions they asked were similar. The shortcuts they refused were familiar. The discomfort they tolerated in pursuit of clarity was shared.

This informal network—often simply referred to as the "TG Tribe"—was neither exclusive nor self-conscious. Its members did not seek recognition as inheritors of a legacy. They demonstrated it through action.

Gupta's legacy also lay in what he refused to do. He did not consolidate power, pursue an empire, or seek permanent relevance. He believed leadership was successful only when it made itself unnecessary. The systems he built were designed to function without him.

Chapter 17 examines this legacy not as nostalgia, but as a consequence. It shows how one individual, by insisting on clarity, discipline, and respect for practice, reshaped an industry without owning it.

In the end, Tarun Gupta's legacy is best understood not as memory, but as momentum—the continuing movement of ideas that still shape decisions long after the man who first articulated them has stepped away.

The TG Tribe: Leaders Across Indian Pharma

The term "TG Tribe" was never coined by Tarun Gupta, nor would he have encouraged it. He was wary of cults, suspicious of labels, and uncomfortable with anything that suggested personal following. Yet over time, the pattern became unmistakable. Across the Indian pharmaceutical industry, leaders emerged who shared a common imprint—one shaped not by allegiance, but by exposure.

Members of the TG Tribe did not announce themselves. They revealed their lineage through behavior. They asked precise questions. They resisted shortcuts. They insisted on clarity where others accepted approximation. In meetings, their focus drifted quickly from opinion to execution. They shared an intolerance for ambiguity that had no owner.

These leaders could be found in competing companies, often across the table from one another. They disagreed vigorously on strategy, yet operated from a similar mental framework. Product management, to them, was not an administrative function but a leadership role. The field was not a cost center; it was the site where credibility was earned or lost. Data was not decorative; it was diagnostic.

What bound the TG Tribe was not loyalty to a man or a company, but adherence to standards. Many had worked directly with Gupta at Glaxo. Others had learned under his students, absorbing principles secondhand. The transmission was subtle but durable.

By the late 1970s and into the decades that followed, this diffusion reached an extraordinary scale. At one point, it was estimated that over half of the marketing leadership shaping the Indian pharmaceutical market had been trained within the Glaxo system, influenced by Gupta. Without coordination or intent, an industry began to speak a shared language.

The Tribe's influence was most evident in what it refused to normalize. Inflated claims, casual ethics, and performative marketing found little traction among its members. Professional dignity mattered. So did preparation. Training was taken seriously. Decisions were expected to withstand scrutiny.

Yet the TG Tribe was not static. Its members adapted to new realities—regulatory change, data evolution, digital transformation. What remained constant was the underlying discipline: a respect for practice, a belief in systems, and a commitment to integrity.

This chapter explores the TG Tribe not as a fraternity, but as a phenomenon. It shows how leadership, when grounded in teaching rather than control, creates influence that travels—quietly, persistently, and at scale.

In tracing these leaders across Indian pharma, the narrative returns to a central insight of Tarun Gupta's career: that the most enduring impact of a leader is not who follows them, but who thinks differently because of them.

Finding Talent Better than Yourself

The Ramanathan Partnership

Tarun Gupta held an unfashionable belief for someone in authority: that leadership is proven not by indispensability, but by replacement. He believed that the ultimate test of a leader was the ability to identify—and then empower—people who could eventually surpass him. The partnership with K. S. Ramanathan stands as the clearest expression of this conviction.

Gupta did not seek likeness. He sought capability. Ramanathan brought a different temperament, a complementary intellect, and a rigor that matched Gupta's own. Where Gupta framed systems, Ramanathan executed with precision. Where Gupta asked expansive questions, Ramanathan enforced discipline. The partnership worked not because of harmony, but because of alignment.

From the outset, Gupta treated Ramanathan not as a subordinate, but as a professional equal in the making. Authority was shared deliberately. Responsibility was real. Ramanathan was entrusted with decisions that mattered, and he was expected to defend them. This was not delegation as convenience; it was delegation as development.

Gupta understood that empowering strong talent requires restraint. He resisted the temptation to intervene unnecessarily. When Ramanathan differed in approach, Gupta listened. When mistakes occurred, they were examined, not punished. The goal was not control, but growth.

The impact of this partnership extended beyond the individuals involved. It set a precedent. Others saw that excellence was not threatening; it was valued. Ambition was not suppressed; it was cultivated. The organization learned that advancement was based on capability, not proximity.

Ramanathan, in turn, deeply absorbed Gupta's philosophy. He carried forward the emphasis on systems, clarity, and respect for execution. Over time, his own leadership reflected these principles, influencing teams and organizations beyond their original context.

Finding talent better than oneself is a rare act of confidence. It requires a leader secure enough to imagine a future in which they are no longer central. Gupta embraced this future willingly.

The Ramanathan partnership captures a defining truth of Tarun Gupta's legacy: that leadership multiplies when it invests in successors who can stand on their own. In choosing strength over control, Gupta ensured that his influence would endure—not through presence, but through people.

Chapter 18

Lessons from the Road not Taken

Wisdom is Knowing when not to Act

Tarun Gupta believed that leadership was tested not only by decisions made but by temptations resisted.

In an environment where growth was often equated with acquisition and expansion, Gupta remained cautious. Opportunities were evaluated rigorously, but not all were pursued. The question he asked was not "Can we?" but "Should we?"—and, just as importantly, "At what cost to clarity and culture?"

Missed acquisitions were not treated as failures. They were regarded as judgments exercised under pressure. Gupta understood that every addition altered an organization's center of gravity. Scale could amplify strength, but it could just as easily dilute discipline.

This restraint was anchored in what he half-jokingly called the Gadhaaram philosophy—a deliberate posture of intellectual humility. To remain a student, he believed, one had to resist certainty, question momentum, and accept that not all paths needed to be explored to be understood.

The Lesson he Left behind was Quiet and Counter-cultural

Leaders who know when not to act protect the integrity of what already works.

In the end, Gupta measured success not by how much was accumulated, but by how carefully coherence was preserved.

Most leadership stories end with triumph. Tarun Gupta's story insisted on something rarer: reflection. He believed that wisdom was not extracted only from success, but from decisions consciously deferred, paths examined and declined. Chapter 18 turns to these moments—not as regrets, but as lessons from the road not taken.

Gupta was acutely aware of opportunity. He saw possibilities long before they became obvious to others. Yet he was equally aware of constraint—

organizational, cultural, and ethical. Not every attractive path, he believed, deserved pursuit. Judgment lay in knowing when restraint was the more disciplined choice.

The missed acquisitions—such as Nicholas and Raptakos, Brett & Co.—are often cited in hindsight as turning points. With time, it is easy to frame them as lost chances. Gupta resisted such simplification. He understood that acquisitions are not merely financial acts; they are integrations of people, systems, and values. Timing mattered. Readiness mattered. Alignment mattered.

What distinguished Gupta's approach was his refusal to romanticize scale. Growth for its own sake held little appeal. He was wary of complexity that diluted standards, of expansion that outpaced capability. In choosing not to proceed, he was protecting something less visible but more valuable: coherence.

These decisions reveal Gupta's broader philosophy of leadership. He believed that leaders are custodians, not conquerors. Their role is to strengthen institutions, not stretch them beyond integrity. Opportunity, in his view, had to be earned through preparation.

The road not taken also extended to personal ambition. Gupta did not pursue perpetual authority. He stepped aside when systems were stable and successors capable. This restraint, too, was deliberate.

Chapter 18 closes the narrative not with certainty, but with humility. Gupta often reminded his students and colleagues that leaders must remain students—that certainty is the enemy of learning. He referred to this stance as the "Gadhaaram" philosophy: the willingness to remain open, questioning, and aware of one's limits.

In reflecting on paths untaken, Tarun Gupta demonstrated that leadership is as much about saying no as it is about saying yes. The lessons lie not in what might have been, but in what was preserved—and in the understanding that wisdom often resides in restraint.

The Missed Acquisitions

Nicholas and Raptakos–Brett

With the benefit of hindsight, it is tempting to view every unrealized acquisition as a lost opportunity. Markets reward scale, and history often celebrates those who expand fastest. Tarun Gupta resisted this retrospective certainty. For him, acquisitions were not trophies to be collected, but commitments that reshaped an organization's character.

The possibilities around Nicholas and Raptakos, Brett & Co., emerged at moments when consolidation in Indian pharmaceuticals was still tentative. Both companies carried strong brands, deep local roots, and the promise of accelerated growth. On paper, the logic was persuasive. Strategically, they offered access. Financially, they were defensible.

Gupta's hesitation was not born of timidity. It was born of judgment.

He understood that acquisition is not an extension of strategy—it is a test of it. Integration demands managerial depth, cultural alignment, and the capacity to absorb complexity without eroding standards. Gupta asked questions others deferred: Who will lead the combined entity? How will systems integrate? What will be lost in the process of gaining scale?

In the case of Nicholas and Raptakos–Brett, Gupta sensed that the organization's internal readiness lagged behind the opportunity. Marketing systems were strong, but leadership bandwidth was finite. Training pipelines were still maturing. He believed that premature expansion risked diluting the very discipline that had made growth possible.

These judgments were unpopular to some. Opportunity, once visible, exerts pressure. Yet Gupta held firm. He preferred coherence to conquest, depth to display.

With time, it became clear that these companies would go on to shape the industry in their own right—through other partnerships and trajectories. The market moved. Others consolidated. History unfolded differently than the spreadsheets once predicted.

Gupta did not revisit these decisions with regret. He saw them as evidence of restraint exercised under temptation. Leadership, he believed, was not about maximizing optionality, but about protecting integrity.

The missed acquisitions of Nicholas and Raptakos–Brett stand as reminders that growth has a rhythm—and that stepping out of tempo can weaken even the strongest organizations. In choosing not to act, Tarun Gupta demonstrated that wisdom sometimes lies not in expansion, but in patience—and that the roads not taken can be as instructive as those pursued.

The "Gadhaaram" Philosophy

Tarun Gupta often used the word "Gadhaaram" with a quiet smile. It was not self-deprecation, nor was it provocation. It was philosophy—compressed into a single, disarming term. In a world that rewarded confidence, certainty, and authority, Gupta chose a posture that ran counter to all three: the willingness to remain a student.

" Gadhaaram," in Gupta's usage, did not mean ignorance. It meant refusal to pretend omniscience. It was an antidote to the arrogance that often accompanies experience. The longer one leads, Gupta believed, the greater the risk of mistaking familiarity for understanding. The Gadhaaram mindset existed to guard against that drift.

Gupta invoked the term when discussions hardened too quickly, when answers arrived too confidently, when learning gave way to performance. Assume you do not know, he would suggest. Begin again. The phrase reset the room.

This philosophy shaped his leadership in subtle but powerful ways. Gupta listened more than he spoke. He questioned even his own convictions. He encouraged disagreement—not as dissent, but as inquiry. The Gadhaaram stance allowed ideas to evolve without ego.

Importantly, it also framed failure differently. Mistakes were not indictments; they were data. One could afford to be wrong if one was willing to learn. This created psychological safety without lowering standards—a rare balance.

In teaching, the philosophy was transformative. Students accustomed to projecting confidence were invited to suspend it. Learning, Gupta insisted, begins at the edge of discomfort. The Gadhaaram mindset legitimized curiosity and protected humility.

In leadership, it fostered adaptability. Markets changed. Science evolved. Regulations tightened. Leaders who clung to certainty struggled. Those who remained Gadhaarams adjusted.

The philosophy also underpinned Gupta's restraint in decision-making—his willingness to defer acquisitions, to step aside when successors were ready, to accept that no system is final. Knowledge, he believed, is provisional.

The "Gadhaaram" philosophy was not a rejection of expertise. It was its refinement. It reminded those around him that wisdom is not accumulation, but openness—and that leadership, at its highest level, requires the courage to admit that learning never ends.

In articulating this idea so simply, Tarun Gupta left behind a final lesson: that the strongest leaders are those who remain willing to begin again.

The TG Principles

A distillation of Tarun Gupta's way of thinking

Tarun Gupta left no manifesto.

What he left behind was a method—visible in how decisions were made, roles were designed, and standards were sustained.

These principles are not slogans. They are working beliefs, repeatedly tested in practice.

1. **Practice Over Proclamation**

   Marketing is not what is said; it is what survives the field.

   Ideas earn respect only after they withstand reality.

2. **Strategy and Execution Are Separate Disciplines**

   Good thinking does not guarantee good action.

   They must be designed, owned, and measured independently—then held in balance.

3. **Clarity Is a Leadership Responsibility**

   Ambiguity breeds conflict.

   When roles, authority, and accountability are clear, politics recedes.

4. **The Field Is a Professional Space**

   Every interaction with a doctor is a moment of judgment.

   Brevity, accuracy, and restraint signal respect.

5. **Products Compete. Categories Endure**

   Brands grow stronger when they define categories, not campaigns.

   Category clarity simplifies execution.

6. **Systems Outlast Individuals**

   Organizations mature when success is reproducible.

   If performance depends on heroics, the system is incomplete.

7. **Recognition Signals Standards**

   What an organization celebrates publicly defines what it values privately.

   Meeting expectations is professional; exceeding them is a distinction.

8. **Training Is Infrastructure, Not a Perk**

   Capability must be reinforced continuously.

   People may leave; standards must not.

9. **Integrity Is Designed, Not Preached**

   Ethical behavior weakens where discretion is vague.

   Clear systems reduce temptation.

10. **Intelligence Must Be Cultivated**

    Experience alone does not sharpen judgment.

    Exposure, writing, and questioning do.

11. **Leadership Is Restraint as Much as Action**

    Every opportunity changes what follows.

    Knowing when not to act preserves coherence.

12. **Legacy Is What Continues Without You**

    True leadership makes itself unnecessary.

    Influence endures when standards travel independently.

13. **Remain a Student**

    Certainty is the enemy of judgment.

    The Gadhaaram stance—intellectual humility—is a discipline, not a pose.

    Tarun Gupta did not aim to be remembered.

    He aimed to be understood.

    These principles endure because they were not declared.

    They were practiced—again and again—until they became a habit.

Appendix

The TG Toolkit

The ideas Tarun Gupta championed were never meant to remain abstract. He believed that philosophy without method was indulgence, and method without philosophy was mechanical. The TG Toolkit brings together the practical instruments through which his thinking was translated into action—simple in form, demanding in application, and enduring in relevance.

This appendix is not a retrospective summary. It is a working manual. Each element reflects Gupta's insistence that good management can be taught, practiced, and refined.

The Strategy–Execution Quadrant

At the heart of Gupta's thinking lay a deceptively simple insight: strategy and execution are independent variables, not sequential steps. The Strategy–Execution Quadrant mapped organizations and individuals across four zones—high strategy/high execution, high strategy/low execution, low strategy/high execution, and low/low.

Gupta used the quadrant as a diagnostic tool. It clarified why brilliant plans failed and why mediocre ideas sometimes succeeded. More importantly, it forced accountability. One could no longer hide weak execution behind strong intent—or excuse poor strategy with hard work.

The quadrant became a shared language, shaping conversations from boardrooms to field reviews.

The 40-Word Detailing Script

Gupta understood that clarity is hardest where complexity is greatest. The 40-word rule imposed discipline on pharmaceutical detailing, forcing representatives to distill a brand's essence into a precise, memorable narrative.

This was not about simplification for its own sake. It was about ensuring minimum viable quality—a baseline below which communication was unacceptable. If a representative could not explain the value of a brand in forty words, Gupta believed they did not understand it.

The rule elevated consistency, reduced noise, and restored respect for the doctor's time.

The Five Steps of Managerial Selection

Gupta distrusted intuition when it masqueraded as judgment. His five-stage selection process brought structure to the identification of future leaders—testing not only competence, but temperament, ethics, and learning capacity.

Each step filtered for a different dimension: capability, curiosity, resilience, discipline, and integrity. The process was rigorous by design. Gupta believed it was kinder to be demanding at the outset than disappointed later.

A Living Toolkit

What unites these tools is not their format, but their intent. They were designed to be used repeatedly, refined continuously, and taught forward. Gupta discouraged reverence. Tools existed to serve thinking, not replace it.

The TG Toolkit stands as the operational backbone of his legacy—a reminder that enduring leadership is built not only on insight, but on systems that make insight actionable.

For readers, this appendix offers more than historical context. It provides instruments still capable of shaping decisions today—true to Gupta's belief that good management, once learned, should travel.

The Strategy–Execution Quadrant

Tarun Gupta was impatient with explanations that treated failure as mysterious. In his experience, outcomes—good or bad—were almost always traceable to a simple imbalance: people either thought well and acted poorly, or acted energetically without thinking clearly. The Strategy–Execution Quadrant emerged as his way of making this imbalance visible.

At its core, the quadrant separates two dimensions that are often mistakenly fused. Strategy is the quality of thinking—clarity of intent, soundness of logic, understanding of the market. Execution is the quality of action—discipline, consistency, follow-through. One does not automatically guarantee the other.

By plotting these dimensions against each other, Gupta created four distinct zones.

Infographic: The Strategy-Execution Quadrant

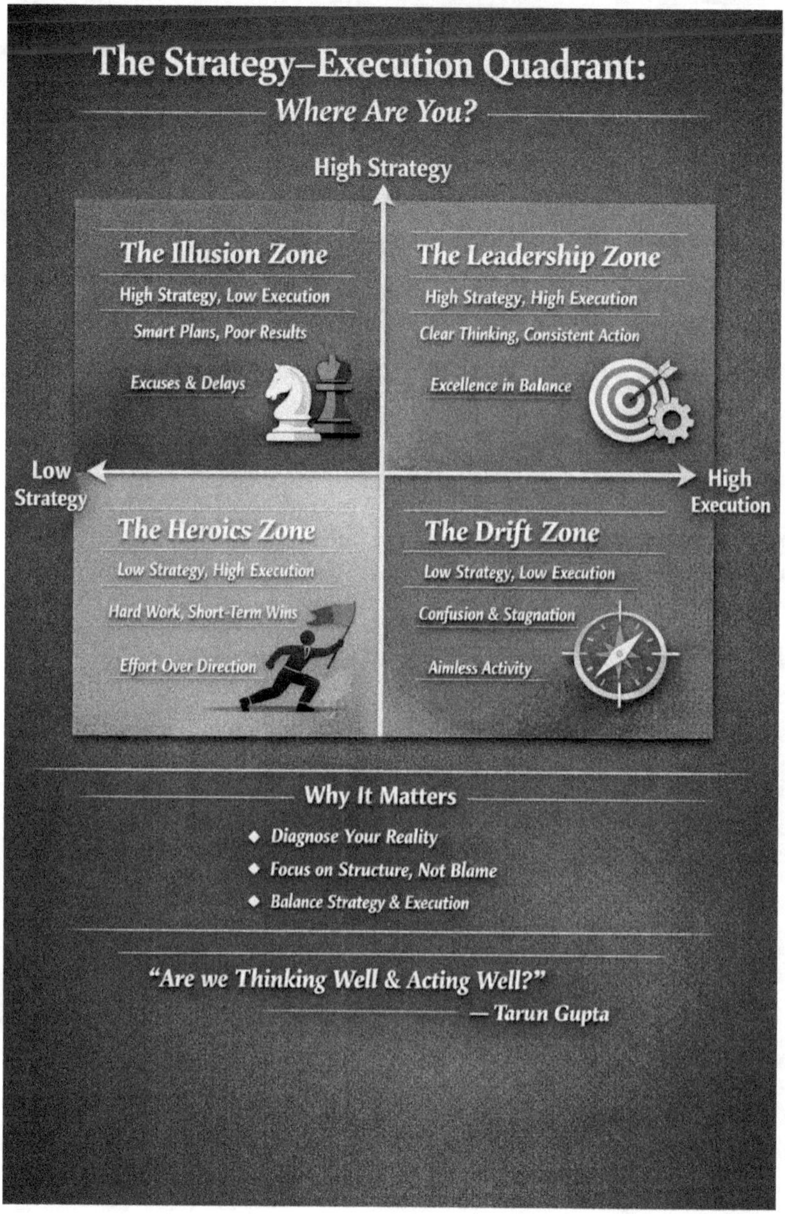

High Strategy / High Execution – The Leadership Zone

This is where organizations aspire to operate. Strategy is coherent and grounded in insight. Execution is disciplined and consistent. Decisions translate into results with minimal leakage. Gupta believed this zone was rare and fragile. It required constant reinforcement, because complacency was its greatest enemy.

Leaders in this quadrant did not confuse brilliance with success. They built systems to ensure that good ideas survived contact with reality.

High Strategy / Low Execution – The Illusion Zone

Here, thinking is sophisticated, presentations impressive, and plans articulate. Yet results disappoint. Gupta encountered this zone often. He referred to it as the most dangerous, because intelligence masks failure. Excuses proliferate. Execution is deferred. Accountability dissolves.

Gupta used the quadrant to confront this illusion directly. If execution was weak, no amount of strategic elegance could compensate.

Low Strategy / High Execution – The Heroics Zone

In this quadrant, energy is abundant but direction is lacking. Teams work hard, targets may be met temporarily, but effort substitutes for clarity. Success depends on individuals rather than systems. Burnout is common. Sustainability is rare.

Gupta respected effort, but he distrusted heroics. He believed that execution without strategy eventually exhausts people and erodes trust.

Low Strategy / Low Execution – The Drift Zone

This was the quadrant Gupta considered most corrosive. There is neither clarity nor discipline. Activity replaces intent. Meetings replace decisions. Organizations here do not fail dramatically—they stagnate.

Gupta saw drift as a leadership failure. The quadrant made such failure undeniable.

Why the Quadrant Mattered?

The power of the Strategy–Execution Quadrant lies in its diagnostic clarity. It removed ambiguity. Teams could locate themselves honestly. Conversations shifted from blame to structure.

Gupta used the quadrant at every level—from individual performance reviews to organizational assessments. It asked one uncompromising question: Are we thinking well, and are we acting well?

The quadrant also reinforced a central belief of Gupta's leadership: that excellence is not accidental. It is engineered through clear thinking and disciplined action, held in balance.

Simple in design and unforgiving in implication, the Strategy–Execution Quadrant remains a fitting distillation of Tarun Gupta's philosophy—one that insists that neither insight nor effort alone is enough, and that leadership resides in the space where the two meet.

The 40-Word Detailing Script

Tarun Gupta believed that clarity was the highest form of respect—especially in the clinic, where time was scarce and attention hard-won. The 40-word detailing script emerged from this belief. It was not a communication trick. It was a discipline designed to reveal whether a brand was truly understood.

Gupta observed that many representatives spoke at length yet said very little. Messages wandered. Claims multiplied. Details obscured purpose. In such encounters, the doctor's patience was consumed, not earned. The 40-word rule imposed a corrective.

The principle was simple and uncompromising: if a representative could not explain the value of a brand in forty words, they did not understand it. The limit forced distillation. Every word had to justify its presence. Redundancy vanished. Jargon was exposed. What remained was essence.

This was not about oversimplification. Gupta insisted that complexity be mastered before it could be reduced. The forty words had to carry scientific credibility, clinical relevance, and differentiation—without exaggeration or noise. The exercise was demanding precisely because it required thinking before speaking.

The script also established minimum viable quality. Regardless of experience or territory, no representative was allowed to fall below this baseline. It ensured consistency without scripting behavior mechanically. Representatives internalized the message, then delivered it in their own voice.

Over time, the 40-word rule reshaped behavior. Preparation improved. Conversations became focused. Doctors sensed the difference immediately. Respect flowed not from verbosity, but from precision.

Gupta also understood the broader implication of the rule. Organizations that cannot articulate their value succinctly often lack strategic clarity. The discipline that improved detailing also sharpened brand strategy and internal alignment.

The 40-word detailing script endures as one of Gupta's most elegant tools. It demonstrated that excellence in communication is not about saying more, but about knowing what must be said—and having the discipline to stop there.

The Five-Step Managerial Selection System

Tarun Gupta distrusted charisma masquerading as leadership. Too often, he observed, organizations promoted their best performers into managerial roles without examining whether they could think, coach, and decide. The five-step managerial selection system was his response—a structured process designed to reduce intuition, expose character, and identify true managerial potential.

The system was rigorous by design. Gupta believed it was kinder to be demanding at the point of selection than corrective after promotion.

Step One: Performance Credibility

The first filter was non-negotiable. Candidates had to demonstrate sustained performance in their current role. Not flashes of brilliance, but consistency. Gupta believed that credibility in execution was the foundation of authority. Without it, leadership lacked legitimacy.

Step Two: Learning Capacity

Gupta valued curiosity as much as competence. Candidates were assessed on their ability to absorb new ideas, question assumptions, and adapt thinking. This was often tested through unfamiliar scenarios rather than rehearsed answers. The goal was to identify minds that could grow.

Step Three: Judgment Under Ambiguity

Management, Gupta insisted, begins where rules end. Candidates were placed in situations with incomplete information and competing priorities. What mattered was not certainty, but reasoning. How did they weigh trade-offs? How did they decide when data was insufficient?

Step Four: People Orientation

Leadership, in Gupta's framework, was inseparable from responsibility for others. Candidates were evaluated on their capacity to coach, listen, and hold people to standards without humiliation. Authority had to be exercised with respect.

Step Five: Integrity and Self-Respect

The final step was the most decisive. Gupta believed that skill without integrity was dangerous. Candidates were observed for consistency between word and action, particularly in small matters. Ethical clarity, once compromised, was difficult to restore.

Why the System Endured?

The five-step system created leaders who shared a common foundation. Promotions were not surprises; they were conclusions. The process reduced favoritism, clarified expectations, and built trust.

More importantly, it aligned leadership selection with Gupta's broader philosophy: that management is not a reward for past success, but a responsibility for future performance.

In institutionalizing this system, Tarun Gupta ensured that leadership quality did not depend on chance. The process itself became a safeguard—one that reflected his belief that good leadership, like good systems, must be designed deliberately.

The TG Principles – Annotated

Tarun Gupta did not articulate his philosophy as doctrine. It emerged through repeated decisions, systems, and standards enforced over time. What follows is an annotated version of the TG Principles, linking each principle to its practical expression in the Indian pharmaceutical industry.

1. **Practice Over Proclamation**

   Principle: Marketing is proven only when ideas survive the field.

   What TG Meant: Grand strategies and elegant presentations had little value unless they could be executed consistently by field teams.

   In Practice: The Digene Gel launch emphasized repetitive, disciplined detailing rather than sporadic high-visibility campaigns. Representatives were required to internalize the story until delivery became natural, not performative.

2. **Strategy and Execution Are Separate Disciplines**

   Principle: Good thinking does not guarantee good action.

   What TG Meant: Strategy is clarity of intent; execution is discipline of follow-through. Confusing the two masks failure.

   In Practice: The Strategy–Execution Quadrant made visible whether organizations were suffering from poor thinking, poor action, or both—removing excuses and forcing diagnosis.

3. **Clarity Is a Leadership Responsibility**

   Principle: Ambiguity creates politics; clarity creates focus.

   What TG Meant: Leaders must design roles and reporting lines so that accountability is structural, not personal.

   In Practice: Eliminating overlapping power centers—such as the redundant All-India Sales Manager role—reduced internal conflict without arbitration.

4. **The Field Is a Professional Space**

   Principle: The clinic is not a stage for performance.

What TG Meant: Doctors' time and judgment must be respected through brevity, accuracy, and restraint.

In Practice: The 40-word detailing rule forced representatives to articulate value succinctly, discouraging exaggeration and waste.

5. **Products Compete. Categories Endure**

   Principle: Brands gain strength when they define categories.

   What TG Meant: Campaigns are temporary; category ownership creates longevity.

   In Practice: Complan was positioned as a solution to growth anxiety, Farex as an entry into responsible infant nutrition, transcending, transcending product features.

6. **Systems Outlast Individuals**

   Principle: Sustainable performance must be reproducible.

   What TG Meant: Reliance on heroics indicates weak systems.

   In Practice: Training, detailing scripts, and review processes ensured consistency even as individuals moved on.

7. **Recognition Signals Standards**

   Principle: What is rewarded publicly defines values privately.

   What TG Meant: Recognition is not motivation; it is communication.

   In Practice: Star Award functions celebrated disciplined achievement, with incentives beginning only beyond 101% performance.

8. **Training Is Infrastructure, Not a Perk**

   Principle: Capability must be reinforced continuously.

   What TG Meant: Attrition is not a reason to stop training.

   In Practice: The ten-year training marathon treated learning as cumulative, not episodic.

9. **Integrity Is Designed, Not Preached**

   Principle: Ethics weaken where systems are vague.

   What TG Meant: Moral exhortation fails without structural clarity.

   In Practice: Point-to-point audits eliminated expense-padding practices without sermons.

10. **Intelligence Must Be Cultivated**

    Principle: Experience alone reinforces habit.

    What TG Meant: Judgment sharpens through exposure and reflection.

    In Practice: Inviting thinkers like Sidney Levy and Gerald Zaltman expanded internal discourse beyond tactics.

11. **Leadership Is Restraint as Much as Action**

    Principle: Not all opportunities deserve pursuit.

    What TG Meant: Scale can dilute coherence.

    In Practice: Missed acquisitions were treated as exercises in judgment, not failure.

12. **Legacy Is What Continues Without You**

    Principle: Influence endures when systems travel independently.

    What TG Meant: Leadership succeeds when it becomes unnecessary.

    In Practice: Former Glaxo-trained managers carried shared standards across competing firms.

13. **Remain a Student (The Gadhaaram Stance)**

    Principle: Intellectual humility preserves judgment.

    What TG Meant: Certainty is the enemy of learning.

    In Practice: TG's insistence on questioning—even late in his career—modeled lifelong learning.

Closing Note: These principles endure not because they were written down, but because they were practiced repeatedly until they became a habit. They form the quiet architecture behind TG's influence.

Bibliography

Marketing Theory, Strategy, and Brand Thinking

1. Levitt, Theodore. "Marketing Myopia." Harvard Business Review 38, no. 4 (July–August 1960): 45–56.
2. Levitt, Theodore. The Marketing Imagination. New York: Free Press, 1983.
3. Kotler, Philip. Marketing Management: Analysis, Planning, and Control. Englewood Cliffs, NJ: Prentice Hall, multiple editions.
4. Keller, Kevin Lane. Strategic Brand Management: Building, Measuring, and Managing Brand Equity. Upper Saddle River, NJ: Pearson Education, multiple editions.
5. Aaker, David A. Managing Brand Equity: Capitalizing on the Value of a Brand Name. New York: Free Press, 1991.
6. Sharp, Byron. How Brands Grow: What Marketers Don't Know. Oxford: Oxford University Press, 2010.

Meaning, Insight, and Consumer Decision Science

1. Levy, Sidney J. "Symbols for Sale." Harvard Business Review 37, no. 4 (July–August 1959): 117–124.
2. Levy, Sidney J. Brands, Consumers, Symbols, and Research. Thousand Oaks, CA: Sage Publications, 1999.
3. Zaltman, Gerald. How Customers Think: Essential Insights into the Mind of the Market. Boston: Harvard Business School Press, 2003.
4. Zaltman, Gerald, and Lindsay Zaltman. Marketing Metaphoria: What Deep Metaphors Reveal about the Minds of Consumers. Boston: Harvard Business School Press, 2008.
5. Kahneman, Daniel. Thinking, Fast and Slow. New York: Farrar, Straus and Giroux, 2011.

Marketing Analytics, Modeling, and Prescription Auditing

1. Little, John D. C. "Models and Managers: The Concept of a Decision Calculus." Management Science 16, no. 8 (April 1970): B466–B485.
2. Little, John D. C., and Philip M. W. Jones. Marketing Engineering. Englewood Cliffs, NJ: Prentice Hall, 2000.
3. Mitra, Chitta. Marketing Research and Analysis. New Delhi: Tata McGraw-Hill, various Indian editions.
4. Green, Paul E., and V. Srinivasan. "Conjoint Analysis in Marketing: New Developments with Implications for Research and Practice." Journal of Marketing 54, no. 4 (October 1990): 3–19.
5. Centre for Marketing Research (C-MARC). Prescription Audit and Panel Data Reports. Mumbai: C-MARC, various years.

Pharmaceutical Marketing and Healthcare Context

1. Kotler, Philip, and Ross L. Clarke. Marketing for Health Care Organizations. Englewood Cliffs, NJ: Prentice Hall, 1987.
2. Smith, Mickey C. Pharmaceutical Marketing Strategy. New York: Pharmaceutical Executive Publications, 1991.
3. IMS Health (now IQVIA). Indian Pharmaceutical Market Overview. Mumbai: IMS Health, various annual reports.
4. Organisation of Pharmaceutical Producers of India (OPPI). Code of Pharmaceutical Practices. Mumbai: OPPI, various editions.
5. Business World. Selected articles on the Indian pharmaceutical industry, 1965–1995.

Management, Leadership, and Organization Design

1. Drucker, Peter F. The Practice of Management. New York: Harper & Row, 1954.
2. Drucker, Peter F. Management: Tasks, Responsibilities, Practices. New York: Harper & Row, 1973.
3. Mintzberg, Henry. The Nature of Managerial Work. New York: Harper & Row, 1973.

4. Mintzberg, Henry. Managers Not MBAs: A Hard Look at the Soft Practice of Managing and Management Development. San Francisco: Berrett-Koehler, 2004.
5. Collins, Jim. Good to Great: Why Some Companies Make the Leap… and Others Don't. New York: HarperBusiness, 2001.

Training, Learning Organizations, and Capability Building

1. Argyris, Chris, and Donald A. Schön. Organizational Learning: A Theory of Action Perspective. Reading, MA: Addison-Wesley, 1978.
2. Senge, Peter M. The Fifth Discipline: The Art and Practice of the Learning Organization. New York: Doubleday, 1990.
3. McCall, Morgan W., Michael M. Lombardo, and Ann M. Morrison. The Lessons of Experience: How Successful Executives Develop on the Job. Lexington, MA: Lexington Books, 1988.
4. Garvin, David A. Learning in Action: A Guide to Putting the Learning Organization to Work. Boston: Harvard Business School Press, 2000.

Ethics, Integrity, and Professional Conduct

1. Badaracco, Joseph L. Defining Moments: When Managers Must Choose between Right and Right. Boston: Harvard Business School Press, 1997.
2. Ciulla, Joanne B. Ethics, the Heart of Leadership. Westport, CT: Praeger, 1998.
3. Treviño, Linda K., and Katherine A. Nelson. Managing Business Ethics: Straight Talk about How to Do It Right. Hoboken, NJ: Wiley, multiple editions.

Management Education and Practice-Based Learning

1. Bennis, Warren G., and James O'Toole. "How Business Schools Lost Their Way." Harvard Business Review 83, no. 5 (May 2005): 96–104.
2. Mintzberg, Henry, and Jonathan Gosling. "Educating Managers Beyond Borders." Academy of Management Learning & Education 1, no. 1 (March 2002): 64–76.
3. The Case Centre. Case Method Teaching Notes. Cranfield, UK: The Case Centre.

4. JBIMS and NMIMS. Archival course material and practice-based teaching notes (unpublished).

Indian Business and Institutional Context

1. Khanna, Tarun. Billions of Entrepreneurs: How China and India Are Reshaping Their Futures—and Yours. Boston: Harvard Business Press, 2007.
2. Das, Gurcharan. India Unbound: From Independence to the Global Information Age. New Delhi: Penguin Books India, 2000.
3. Murthy, N. R. Narayana. A Better India, A Better World. New Delhi: Penguin Random House India, 2015.

Primary and Interpretive Sources

1. Gupta, Tarun. Professional lectures, training notes, and internal presentations (unpublished).
2. "Dr. Tarun Gupta: The Phenomenon Called TG." Obituary and archival tribute document.
3. Interviews, recollections, and professional memory shared by former Glaxo executives, students, and colleagues (1965–1995).

Bibliographic Note

This bibliography presents the conceptual foundations, professional context, and intellectual influences that inform this book.

The work itself is interpretive and practice-oriented, relying on publicly available material, professional memory, and applied judgment rather than proprietary documents.

About the Author

Subba Rao Chaganti is a pioneering voice at the intersection of pharmaceutical marketing, behavioral science, and emerging technologies. With over three decades of industry experience and a prolific portfolio of 29 groundbreaking books on pharmaceutical strategy, Chaganti is widely regarded as a thought leader who redefines how pharma educates, engages, and empowers.

He began his journey as a marketing educator and practitioner, driven by a singular mission: to bridge the gap between science and storytelling in pharma. Today, his work spans disciplines—from sales force effectiveness and key account management to digital therapeutics, wearable tech, internal branding, and AI-powered brand strategy.

Beyond the books, Chaganti is a mentor to brand managers, a respected voice on LinkedIn and Substack, and an unwavering advocate for ethical, patient-centered innovation in life sciences marketing. His ability to translate complexity into actionable strategy makes his work not just readable—but indispensable.

He lives in Farmington, Connecticut, USA, and can be reached at: subbarao.chaganti@gmail.com.

Here is a list of his publications:

1. Pharmaceutical Marketing in India for Today and Tomorrow: 25th Anniversary Edition
2. Game Plans for the Post-GATT Era: Action Agenda of the Indian Pharmaceutical Industry
3. Compete or Forfeit: Strategies for Sustainable Competitive Advantage
4. Bullseyes and Blunders: Lessons from 100 Cases in Pharmaceutical Marketing

5. Digital Pharma Marketing Playbook: Winning with the New Rules of Engagement
6. Cracking the Generics Code: Your Single-Source Success Manual for Winning in Multi-Source Product Markets
7. Reimagine Pharma Marketing: Make it Future-Proof!
8. Brand Positioning in Pharma
9. Transactional to Transformational Marketing in Pharma: The Science of Why and the Art of How
10. A to Z of Pharmaceutical Marketing: World's First and Only Encyclopedia in Two Volumes
11. The Synergy of Minds: Human + AI Orchestrating the Pharma Marketing Revolution
12. Design Thinking for Pharma
13. The Pharma Product Manager: Navigating the Digital Frontier
14. Sentimental Analysis for Pharma Marketers
15. Whispering to AI: Prompt Engineering for Pharma Brand Managers
16. Storytelling in Pharma Marketing
17. Beyond the Molecule: The Art and Science of Metaphors that Matter
18. The Voices Within: Your Body Speaks, When your organs tell their own stories
19. Pharma Archetypes: The Science of Meaningful Healthcare Marketing
20. Navigating the AI Revolution: Human Futures
21. Breaking Through: A Business Novel (based on the theory of constraints)
22. The Wearable Edge: Redefining Pharma Marketing in a Connected and Data Driven World
23. Code to Cure: Digital Therapeutics and the Future of Pharma
24. Level Up: Gamification in Pharma Marketing
25. The Inner Game of Marketing: Mastering the Mind Behind the Message
26. Marketing Fundamentals
27. The Digital Marketer's Playbook

www.ingramcontent.com/pod-product-compliance
Lightning Source LLC
Chambersburg PA
CBHW071447230926
51846CB00001B/373
9789347311765